feelings

EXPLORING YOUR
INNER EMOTIONS

By the same author:

Positive Action for Health and Wellbeing (Class Publishing,
2001, first published in 1987 as *All in the Mind*)
Personal Therapy (Vermillion, 1996, first published in 1989
as *A Safer Place to Cry*)
The Confidence to Be Yourself (Piatkus, 1998)
Understanding Hypnosis (Piatkus, 2000)

feelings

EXPLORING YOUR INNER EMOTIONS

Dr Brian Roet

PIATKUS

First published in 2003 by
Judy Piatkus (Publishers) Limited
5 Windmill Street
London W1T 2JA
e-mail: info@piatkus.co.uk

ISBN 0 7499 2376 8
Illustrated by Georgie Birkett (cartoons) and Rodney Paull
Edited by Trish Burgess
Text design by Briony Chappell, Goldust Design

This book has been printed on paper manufactured
with respect for the environment using wood from
managed sustainable resources

Typeset by Palimpsest Book Production Limited,
Polmont, Stirlingshire
Printed and bound in Denmark by
Nørhaven Paperbacks A/S, Viborg

To Val

Emotion Probably no other term in psychology shares its non-definability with its frequency of use.

Penguin Dictionary of Psychology

Contents

Acknowledgements

I would like to thank Tracey for the tireless job she did in transforming my illegible handwritten manuscript into pristine typed pages.

I would also like to thank Patrick for his ability to change child-like phrases into well-constructed grammar and syntax; Ashley and Neela for their helpful suggestions during a Chinese meal; Fiona, whose tenacity and computer skills helped me achieve the publisher's deadline; Anna, for her calming influence during the publication process; and lastly all those people who answered my strange and often intrusive questions about their personal emotions.

Introduction

Many years ago I was having a variety of problems and sought help from a therapist. In the first session I related an incident that had occurred.

> 'And how do you feel about that Brian?' he asked.
> 'I think it was rather interesting,' I replied.
> 'No. How did you feel about it?' he repeated.
> 'As I said, I think it was interesting,' I again replied.
> 'I'm asking you about your feelings, Brian. What do you feel about that incident?'

I was stunned, silent for a long time.

'I really don't know what you are talking about,' I answered him with all honesty. I knew the word 'feelings' but I had no idea what feelings were.

I have come some way since then, but my head still rules my heart to some degree.

You may well ask, 'How does someone once so bereft of emotions come to be writing a book about them?' Perhaps being an observer allows me to see and query things accepted by others, just as a coach notices things unobserved by the team. It has been said that the spectator sees most of the game.

Emotions are varied and complex parts of our lives, and each person translates them in a different way. Like fingerprints, they are universal yet individually unique. To some they are as easy and natural as breathing, while others struggle with their feelings as an asthmatic gasps for air.

The aim of this book is to help you, the reader, to examine

your emotional make-up and the role this plays in your attitudes and responses to life. I believe the insights you acquire will help you to live more peacefully with yourself and those around you. Like any part of the mind/body system, having the components work well together enables you to perform much more comfortably and successfully.

By working *with* feelings rather than battling against them, we can utilise their power and energy as resources to improve our lives. Doing the best we can allows us to be who we really are, rather than distorting our personality with internal conflicts. Working in harmony with emotions allows us to achieve our greatest potential.

Writing this book has helped me to view the workings of the heart with more importance, and I hope it will do the same for you. It draws on my 30 years of experience in analysis, during which hundreds of clients have consulted me for help with their emotions. Every day I am presented with stories, experiences and difficulties, and my job is to help unravel the tangle causing so much pain. These consultations have provided me with a vast amount of experience – real, not theoretical – in dealing with emotions, and that is the foundation of this book. Already it has met with great success as I have given specific chapters to clients struggling with emotional conflict. Martha, for example, suffered from panic attacks when visiting certain parts of London which triggered memories relating to unpleasant experiences in the past. I gave her the relevant chapter and she was able to 'break her triggers' and travel to those places feeling calm and confident. Similarly, Lucas and his partner read about the art of listening and, as a result, found that their communication and understanding of each other improved immensely.

To gain the most from this book, read it slowly. As it is the distillation of 30 years' experience, treat it like a concentrated cordial. Dilute it by sipping one paragraph, one page, one chapter at a time: digest the words and apply the thoughts to your life. Hurrying through to reach the end is like drinking neat cordial – it will not quench your thirst.

Go back to different sections from time to time and re-read

chapters relating to your needs. You may have progressed since first reading them and be able to make more sense of them the second or third time round.

As you read this book, you will come to understand more about the things we call feelings or emotions, and in the process learn how you can be in harmony with your own emotions rather than being ruled or restricted by them. The connecting thread will take you along labyrinthine passages involving the past and the future, along apparently unrelated pathways, such as belief systems and body language, into concealed caves of the unconscious and laboratories of research scientists. Along the way you will learn about therapies that improve the processing of emotions, techniques such as visualisation that enable you to see feelings inside you, and body manipulation, such as solar plexus pressure, that releases emotions previously undiscovered.

The aim of the book is to help people from all walks of life to understand (and correct) the pattern or sequence of their behaviours. Look at the examples below.

Tom had broken up from his girlfriend Julie one year prior to seeing me, but couldn't get over her. Every waking moment she was there, somewhere inside him, causing grief. Often in our sessions he was bright and cheerful, but when Julie's name was mentioned tears filled his eyes beyond control.

The simplified sequence of events for Tom was:
1) He was feeling bright and cheerful.
2) Julie's name was spoken.
3) His mind processed the word.
4) A feeling was produced.
5) His lachrymal glands were activated.
6) Tears overflowed onto his cheeks.
Tom had no control over the sequence.

Josephine has her specific problems when shopping.
1) She picks up a basket in the supermarket.

2) She experiences the sights, smells and sounds of a normal supermarket.
3) Her mind processes these senses.
4) She is overwhelmed by a feeling of fear.
5) She is unable to do her shopping and leaves.
Josephine has no control of this sequence.

Wendy knows she doesn't want to visit her father who sexually abused her as a child.
1) She receives a call from him inviting her to dinner.
2) She hears his voice, her mind processes what he says and she is unable to say no.
3) From the time of the telephone conversation till the dinner she is in complete turmoil.
4) She attends the dinner, sitting mutely through the meal, paralysed by fear and numb to any other emotion.
Wendy has no control of this sequence of events.

This book is written for the millions of people like Tom, Josephine and Wendy. In fact, everyone has a sequence of events that in some way resembles those just described. How often do we hear, 'I can't do that, I'd be too frightened' or 'I wish I could feel less guilty about doing that' or 'My jealousy ruins every relationship I have'?

Many people are dominated by their emotions in ways that are painful, restrictive and limiting. Choices are not available to them. What they want to do and what they are actually able to do are very separate things. By understanding these mysterious entities called feelings we may well be able to free ourselves from their limiting control. By learning about the ways and means they have to influence our lives, we can ensure they are up to date, appropriate and helpful. By devising techniques to help us improve our feelings and form a useful partnership with them we gain control of our lives.

Emotions are part of a chain reaction involving external events, thoughts, triggers and stored experiences, and by looking at each link of the chain, we begin to understand what is happening. By improving some of these links we create a much more flexible and healthy chain that is supportive rather than restrictive.

Information and understanding impart the power to decide, make choices and direct our lives. My research, as described in this book, will provide you with some of that information and understanding.

So many patients start their consultation with 'Doctor, I feel –' The emotion may be fear, anger, guilt, sadness, jealousy or depression, but the common factor is feelings. Often these feelings are felt in the present but originate in the past. Stored, unresolved emotions lie deep in our unconscious and are brought to life by a variety of factors called 'triggers'. Learning about the original emotions, as well as the triggers, gives us the tools for change.

Emotions have been studied from vastly different perspectives. In 1872 Charles Darwin wrote about emotions in different societies from an evolutionary angle. Sigmund Freud studied the emotions of his patients from a medical point of view, forming theories that became the foundation of psychoanalysis. Modern research using computer-operated imaging devices and molecular studies is currently studying the building blocks of emotion. My aim is to look at emotion from a practical point of view and ask questions that arise from it. Tom's tears, for example, prompt me to ask, 'What is happening now? How can the process be improved? What tools can I provide to enable him to make a change? How can he connect his logic and emotion?'

Many difficulties arise when we try to analyse something so intangible as an emotion. It is a little like catching a moonbeam and placing it in a jar. We cannot dissect it on an operating table, see it through a microscope or take an x-ray of it. We only have the patients' words for what is happening inside them, and these are often inadequate to describe what is felt.

To get the most from this book you need to focus on your emotions and the situations where they cause you difficulty. Make use of the examples and case histories, become aware of what is happening inside you and note the process that creates your feelings.

Learn to differentiate between helpful and unhelpful emotions – those that increase your pleasure and those that restrict it. Be open to discussing your feelings with others and listen to their comments. Respect those emotions that are helpful and diminish those that are not.

The heart is traditionally the seat of emotion. Recently I saw a truly amazing sight on television, one I would never have believed possible when I was a young doctor in Australia. A man was presenting *his heart* in a jar to the Science Museum. He was a transplant patient and his malfunctioning heart was in the jar while a new, healthy heart was beating in his chest.

Perhaps the aim of this book is to help you be like that man, and replace unhealthy emotions with those that will support you for the rest of your life.

PART I

What Are Emotions?

1
Emotions, Feelings and Moods

'Everything is about something different.'
VARINDRA VITTACHI, JOURNALIST AND AUTHOR

Six blindfolded men were asked to feel different parts of an animal and describe what sort of animal it might be. They were led to an elephant (an animal none of them had seen before); one was directed to feel the trunk, another the ears, another the tusks, another the feet, another the body and the last the tail. Not surprisingly, their descriptions differed hugely because of the very different information they received. In order to obtain an accurate description of the animal they would need to pool their knowledge and fit their impressions together in a logical way.

So it is with emotions. To define what they are requires many pieces of information to be correctly collated. As scientific research improves, more pieces are becoming apparent, but the process of piecing them together is still in progress.

This chapter examines moods, feelings, temperament and emotions, defining what they mean in simple terms and exploring where they originate. This information will help you to arrive at a clearer understanding of the physiology of emotions. In the process, it will also provide insights to your own emotional make-up.

In the past, analysis of emotions was thought to be unscientific because they were subjective, existing as a perceived entity rather than a measurable one. The scientific view was, 'If you can't measure it, it cannot be evaluated.'

Now, with modern technology, research into emotions occupies the minds and laboratories of scientists around the world. Because data is being collated and is reproducible, emotional research is taking its rightful place in the expansion of our understanding of human beings.

As with the elephant, emotions can be viewed from a variety of perspectives – evolutionary, molecular, biological, genetic and psychological to name just a few. Before we go along these pathways it is important to understand what is meant by 'emotion'. The word is derived from the Latin prefix *e*, meaning 'away' and *movere* meaning 'to move'. This 'moving away' implies that emotions result in actions, such as shyness leading to withdrawal, and fear leading to flight.

The text that follows offers simple explanations of some of the terms used when emotions are discussed.

Moods

Moods occur as background feelings and may last hours or days. They are not necessarily triggered by a specific event, but they alter our susceptibility to emotional stimuli. If we are in a bad mood and hear sad news, we will be more upset than if we are in a good mood and receive the same news.

We often talk about moods, offering them as an explanation for our behaviour. We may wake up in a bad mood ('I got out of bed on the wrong side this morning'), being aware that our day will be influenced by this. We don't seek a rational explanation, and generally none is on offer.

Moods may be likened to deep currents, while emotions are represented by waves. Moods may well be the result of hormonal changes, unconscious recall, dreams, past experiences, or they may 'just happen'. We may have a 'moody temperament' that lends itself to mood swings, or be predominantly pessimistic or optimistic, leading others to remark, 'He's always in a bad (good) mood.'

Body language is an external sign of the processes occurring inside us. At a glance it is often possible to tell if someone is tense, gloomy, relaxed or irritable, even if you've never met before.

Feelings

Feelings are what we feel. They are the bodily sensations we experience in response to an emotion. These may include changes in muscle tension, heart rate, sweat gland activity, body temperature, pupil dilation and skin colour, the degree of change being directly related to the intensity of the emotion. When we become aware of these changes we are 'feeling'.

The words used to describe feelings – worried, embarrassed, hurt, upset, remorseful, vulnerable and shy, for example – all imply the bodily sensations we experience in response to our moods or emotions. Outsiders may or may not be able to deduce what we are feeling as our feelings are internal private affairs.

Temperament

Temperament may be defined as the predominant nature or character of a person. It relates to a basic, more fixed aspect of personality, such as optimism or violence, that we may have inherited from our parents or grandparents. This is illustrated by such comments as: 'I'm such a moody person, just like my dad,' or 'I've always had a happy disposition, ever since kindergarten days.'

Upbringing may play a role in determining temperament, but the most likely influence is our genetic make-up. As a rule, temperament is more likely to be modified by experience rather than changed.

Emotions

Human beings have had emotions since the beginning of time, but it is only over the last century or so that we have arrived at a rational, scientific understanding of this mind/body process that affects us so profoundly.

Emotions are even more complex than moods, feelings or temperament. Just as the six blindfolded men at the beginning of this chapter would need to pool their findings in order to construct the likeness of an elephant, so we need to look at the complexities of emotion from a variety of vantage points to recognise its real character.

The American psychology professor Robert Pluchik has identified eight primary emotions – sadness, disgust, anger, anticipation, joy, acceptance, fear and surprise. These, like primary colours, can be blended to form secondary emotions. For example, joy + fear = guilt, while anger + joy + fear = guilt.

Primary emotions are intense, they take over our mind/body system and override rationality. What is the benefit of having one system dominate another? The answer may lie in a future outcome or in the evolutionary past. As emotions were part of mammalian life long before the rational brain cortex developed, their power may simply be due to the fact that they were there first.

The evolution of emotions

The evolutionary importance of emotions was acknowledged by Charles Darwin in 1872 when he wrote a book called *The Expression of the Emotions in Man and Animals*. Having studied different tribes from around the world, he found that facial expressions in response to specific emotions were very similar. He also noted that facial expressions of different animals utilised similar muscles to man when expressing similar emotions. This, he concluded, provided evidence that man descended from animals.

In recent years Paul Ekman, an American psychologist studying human emotion, performed similar research by showing various ethnic groups around the world photographs of people demonstrating sadness, disgust, anger, joy, surprise and fear. Some of these groups had never seen a white person before but they all recognised facial expressions and the emotions they were illustrating.

Human beings and animals share many responses to emotion, such as the eyes widening with fear and the skin changing colour with anger. This has more to do with survival than empathy. Animals need to feel fear and recognise the body language of other animals so that they can escape predators or convey useful information, such as disgust at inedible food or anger at threats to security.

As time has passed emotional responses in human beings have been refined so that social interactions are more finely tuned than they were with animals, but evolution has not always kept pace with social change. Part of the emotional circuit lies in a primitive part of our brain, and the pattern of response dates back millions of years. What was useful for a prehistoric man may not be useful for a human being in the 21st century, but we're saddled with the response because that's the way we're 'built'.

When cave man felt trapped by a predator the fight-or-flight response enabled him to deal with the situation and survive. If 21st-century man is trapped in a traffic jam the same neuro-chemical response occurs but there is no benefit in hitting the driver of the car in front or running away, although that is what our neurochemical response is telling us to do.

The anatomy of emotions

Anatomical structures involved with emotions are directly related to the evolutionary process. The most primitive part of the brain – the brain stem or reptilian brain – is an extension of the spinal cord into the skull. It is responsible for basic and essential functions such as breathing, heart rate, temperature control, bowel and kidney function and reflex responses.

Millions of years after the brain stem formed, a ring of nerves called the limbic system evolved to encircle the brain stem. This system brought memory, learning and emotions to mammals that existed 100 million years ago, so it could be called the 'emotional brain'.

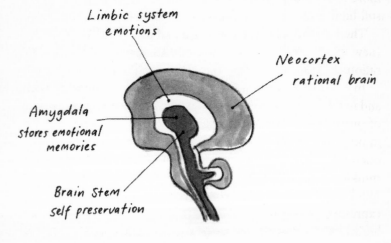

Anatomy of emotions

An important part of the emotional brain is the amygdala, which contains the blueprint of childhood experiences and causes the adult responses that follow. It is the storehouse of emotional memory, and often one word overpowers our rational thought processes. When rage, jealousy or obsessive fear overcome our logical mind, the amygdala is involved.

As a survival mechanism, the amygdala 'scans' past experiences and 'matches' them with present-day situations. As the scanning needs to be instantaneous to provide protection, there is often a 'mismatch' between the original and present-day situations, and problems arise when out-of-date responses are triggered.

For example, if someone's life has been threatened by a tall man with a moustache, it is possible that later scanning and matching in the amygdala will create terror when a similar person is seen, even though the logical mind knows this person to be harmless. Because the emotional brain was present millions of years before the rational brain existed, its influence is very powerful. Although evolution may allow us to develop more abilities and flexibilities, more choices, more information and more tools to deal with challenges, basic emotional powers may still hold sway.

The last part of the brain to develop is called the neocortex (new outer layer). This covers the brain and is responsible for rational thinking, intellect and logic.

In addition to the brain, we also have a vast network of nerves and nervous connections (synapses) involved in the transmission of our feelings. Past researchers believed rationality was in the mind and emotions in the body. More recently scientists thought one part of the brain was used for emotions and another for thinking. Now we postulate a mind/body complex, where both mind and body are integral components for the creation and expression of emotion. The connections between the emotional brain and emotional body combine to form an integrated system.

Research into emotion

In an effort to understand the enigma of emotions, many research programmes focus on specific parts of the brain where disease or trauma have produced circumscribed damage. By studying the response of people with such conditions we learn how different parts of the brain function. The responses of laboratory animals following emotional triggers also add to our knowledge about the 'system of emotions'.

Many facets of emotion – chemical, hormonal, cognitive, neurological, evolutionary – are now being studied. The information gathered is gradually being pieced together to form 'the big picture', and psychologist Paul Ekman has formulated a theory called the 'affect program'. This states that emotions are *complex* because they affect so many parts of the body, *co-ordinated* because they occur in patterns or sequences, and *automated* because they occur without the need for conscious direction.

The chemical view of emotions

In her book *The Molecules of Emotion* neuroscientist Candice Pert discusses the role body chemicals play in the formation and transmission of emotion. In the 1970s she discovered a method of measuring 'receptor sites' – parts of cell membranes that allow certain molecules to attach and create chemical changes.

The chemical changes resulting from molecular binding at receptor sites create moods and emotions. Very specific changes occur depending on the molecule attaching and the individual receptor site. The process resembles a jigsaw in that only certain molecules can attach to sites where binding occurs.

The specific molecules involved with the transmission and formation of emotions are called neuropeptides. Their function is to distribute information throughout the body by travelling to specific receptor sites. Some go to the lining of blood vessels to alter bloodflow, others reach the gut and change the mobility of the bowel, still others affect muscular tension.

In 1920 a neurosurgeon called William Penfold stimulated different parts of the brain during surgery while the patient was awake. He was able to produce intense emotions such as rage and grief when he stimulated different areas. The electric stimulus re-awoke memories of past experiences by releasing neuropeptides, which then attached to specific receptor sites.

Further research demonstrated large stores of neuropeptides occurring at different sites in both the brain and body. These sites, where a great deal of information converged, were called nodal points (or hotspots). The fact that they occurred in both the brain and the body was further evidence that emotions involved the total mind/body complex. These molecular-receptor systems are concerned with production, storage and transmission of emotion.

As a result of past experiences, we develop a unique filtering system that affects the way neuropeptides move and attach to receptor sites. This filtering system explains how two individuals experiencing the same stimulus may feel completely differently. It is as if the body remembers and influences the present-day event using chemicals related to past experience.

Neuropeptides – the smallest components of emotional production – are produced by many different parts of the mind/body complex. They are categorised by the different actions they perform – neurotransmitters, growth factors and hormones, for example. Collectively they are called informational substances.

The flow of these substances is very important in regulating bodily systems. Stress, pressure and tension alter this flow, causing incorrect distribution, which can lead to problems with breathing, bloodflow, the immune system and digestion.

When stress blocks the flow of these substances they are stored at a cellular level in the form of 'repressed emotions'. These are not easily available for release, but affect our perspective by creating an out-of-date filter that colours our point of view.

Some people believe that we feel happy when our informational molecules are flowing freely to open receptors. This allows integration and co-ordination of the many systems in the mind/body complex. By expressing emotions, sharing them and being listened to we are aiding the flow of informational substances and allowing receptors to be open to receive more molecules. By denying or repressing emotions the network of pathways is blocked and distorted, reducing the flow of 'feel-good' chemicals.

Pathways of the emotions

While emotions travel through the mind and body via the blood-stream, they are also conveyed via the nervous system. This intricate web of nerves, nerve cells, connecting synapses and ganglia conveys messages through nervous impulses which affect the 'end organs', such as blood vessels, skin, heart and gut.

The initial stimulus is caused by our senses of touch, sight, hearing, smell and taste. These cause nervous impulses to be conveyed through the network of nerve fibres, which in turn release neuropeptides. These neuropeptides circulate through the bloodstream to arrive at specific receptor sites, where they create chemical changes that result in emotions.

Because there is an intimate relationship between the nervous impulses and the neurotransmitters, and because neuropeptides are found in both brain and body, it is now believed that emotions originate in both the mind and the body.

Displays of emotion

By observing animals we can see that there is a wide variety of body languages displayed in different situations. A bird defending its territory, for example, has a different song and behaviour than it uses during the mating season or when it is cornered and under attack. These behaviours, which include bodily changes, alteration in colour and modification of call, are all external manifestations of internal emotions. What we see is a reflection of what is felt.

In a less vivid way the same occurs in humans, as we have inherited these tendencies through the evolutionary process. We may not exhibit vast colour changes, have our hair stand on end or hop on one leg, but we certainly illustrate our emotions with body language. For example, researchers have discovered that we blush very slightly under our eyes when we tell a lie. Infrared cameras measuring heat change can detect this blushing when subjects lie, so modern lie-detector tests make use of this response.

Using body language to send information to others about our emotional state is a very important form of communication. It allows them to gain knowledge without it being distorted by our intellectual system. These display messages allow us to determine the attitude of someone even if it differs markedly from the words they use. For example, if someone goes red in the face, tightens the jaw or clenches the fists when saying 'I love my mother', we would tend to believe their body language rather than their words.

Consciousness of emotions

On an emotional level humans differ from animals because we know that we have feelings. Being conscious of our emotions allows us an element of control: by knowing how we feel, we are in a position to learn how to respond to the feeling.

'I am angry and I know that I am angry' gives me more choices in how to deal with my anger than if I was just angry. Knowing how we feel and knowing what caused that feeling does not necessarily mean we can change the emotional response. If you are frightened of flying and know why you are frightened of flying, this does not mean you can stop being frightened, but it enables you to take steps to avoid that feeling – something you couldn't do if you didn't know how you felt.

Many emotions occur beyond our conscious awareness. We may radiate anger because the neuropeptide transmission for anger is occurring, but be aware and refute it when others comment. The feelings are not felt by the conscious mind. Whether a feeling is felt or not depends on many factors, including past experiences and memory. Because emotion was part of our evolutionary process long before consciousness appeared, it is understandable how many emotions remain beyond the reach of reason. When we do become aware of our feelings, this awareness affects them and may create a different feeling, and so the tapestry of emotions and thoughts is continually being re-woven.

Cultural differences in emotions

It is obvious to anyone who travels that there is a cultural norm expressing the attitudes and behaviour of people in the country visited. Emotional responses vary greatly from country to country, and behaviour accepted in one may be rejected in another. For example, a stiff upper lip in times of stress is much admired by the British, but other cultures perceive this behaviour as cold and heartless. In some countries, expressions of emotion are expected and encouraged, hence the noisy weeping and wailing at Middle Eastern funerals.

Neither of these examples is correct or incorrect behaviour. The important thing to remember is that expressing emotions as they are felt is more in harmony with the needs of our mind/body system than repressing them or expressing them theatrically.

Learning about emotions

The aim of this book is to remove the blindfolds from those trying to understand the elephant of emotion. The following chapters will help you to understand at different levels how emotion plays a major part in our lives. Knowing that a feeling is the distribution of a neuropeptide to a receptor cell does not help in dealing with that feeling. However, gaining insight into the origins of emotions helps us realise that complex processes are involved when feelings take over.

By being aware of the way you feel, and learning what has produced that feeling, you are in a strong position to do something about it. As you read this book you will become more and more aware of your own feelings, how they influence you and how to improve their function. You will in fact be altering the emotional molecules circulating inside you.

Note: Because there is a continuum between moods, feelings and emotions – one flowing into the other – I have taken the liberty throughout this book of using these terms interchangeably. This is not strictly accurate scientifically but makes for less confusion and easier reading.

2

Why Do We Have Emotions?

'For sweet, to feel is better than to know, and wisdom is a
childless heritage, One pulse of passion – youth's first fiery glow –
are worth the hoarded proverbs of the sage.'

OSCAR WILDE, *PANTHEA*

The question 'Why do we have emotions?' is impossible to answer
definitively. We can postulate, using ideas evolved from science,
philosophy and art, but in the end it will still be a postulation.
In order to pursue the question further we need to look at the
role emotions play in our lives. We need to observe the benefits
gained by displaying them, and study those who have lost the
ability to do so because of physical or psychological damage.
This chapter presents that information with the aim of helping
you to understand and, to some extent, control your own
emotional responses.

The search for why we have emotions is based more on practical evidence than intellectual facts. Emotions have been passed
down from generation to generation, so it is reasonable to
assume they play a major function in our survival. Some of the
emotions essential to prehistoric animals are still with us, but
the role they play is no longer related to life and death issues.

Although culture and learning can give emotions new
meaning, or modify our expression of them, the fact is that
emotions are biologically determined processes, depending on
set brain devices laid down by our evolutionary history.

Emotions lead us to action – either towards or away from the stimulus. The 'why' of emotion is in some way related to this action, whether it be psychological or physical: anger leads us to argue, shyness to retreat, joy to exclaim and embrace, disgust to reject.

For some people emotions are the major currency of life: 'Without my feelings I'd be nothing: life wouldn't be worth living. It would be like existing in black and white rather than Technicolor.'

Others may differ: 'Emotions have ruined my life. I've lost my job and wife because I was overcome with feelings I could not control.'

Emotions can be viewed as energy, which can be constructive or destructive. Problems arise when we are overwhelmed by emotions and lose the balancing power of rationality.

A very useful question to ask yourself is: 'Does this emotion move me forward or does it hold me back?' This will help you to evaluate your feelings and make progress rather than remaining stuck in a rut. Feelings are not bad or good, right or wrong, negative or positive: they are either helpful or unhelpful.

Feelings that move us on are those that add to our lives, enhance our successes and enrich our appreciation. They become a form of information, power and energy that encourages us to proceed along a pathway of our choice. Feelings that hold us back are exactly the opposite.

If you wish to go on holiday, feel invigorated by the preparation and joyous about the prospect of what you will encounter, these feelings are moving you in the direction you wish to go – on holiday.

If, however, you feel guilty about going, frightened of flying and lonely about the time you might be spending on your own, these feelings are holding you back and are contrary to your intention of having a holiday.

While it might be true to say 'We are what we think,' it is also true to say 'We are what we feel,' as it is often our feelings that determine how we respond to the various situations that confront us day to day. It would therefore be even more accurate to say 'We are what we feel and what we think.'

Emotions as Information

Feelings provide us with messages that differ from those we receive from reason. The head and the heart are continually telling us about ourselves, our surroundings, the tasks we need to perform, the pressures exerted upon us, relationships near and far, responsibilities and so forth. These messages are stimuli indicating that action needs to be taken, but the heart and head may have different agendas.

When we think one thing and feel another, we are being provided with two choices. For example, you want a holiday but you feel worried about taking time off. You have to choose between doing yourself some good or dedicating yourself to work. Considering the situation using head and heart is better than using head alone.

In order to be the best source of information, emotions need to be mature, and this depends on how we were treated as children. If we have received good parenting, with love, support, praise, care, guidance and understanding, we develop into mature adults. If these qualities are absent, the child goes astray, adult maturity is not attained and problems occur.

So it is with emotions. Like young children, they need caring for. If we neglect, distort, suppress, block or ignore our emotions they will not reach maturity and will hold us back rather than moving us forward. We will have juvenile, out-of-date, inappropriate or excessive emotions that become restrictive rather than enhancing.

The information-giving aspect of our feelings derives largely from parental example. I see many people who learnt in childhood to criticise, blame, distrust, misunderstand and negate their feelings, and who continue to do so as adults. These people are at war with their feelings, and their feelings are at war with them. It is no wonder that the emotional information received by such people is greatly distorted and unhelpful.

The mind/heart partnership has three components: our rational thoughts, our emotions, and our conscious awareness of our emotions (knowing how we feel). When we possess all three interacting in a healthy state, we are in the best possible position to deal with the world.

Studies of people or animals who are deficient in one or more of these components illustrate how we behave when the system is out of balance.

Case History

Michael climbed a tree to disentangle a kite. He fell to the ground, hitting his head on a rock and damaging part of the left frontal lobe of his brain. This contained part of his reasoning system, so the three components of the mind/heart partnership were thrown out of balance, allowing his emotion to have free rein.

Michael cried and laughed following minimal stimuli, gave his possessions away at a whim, and reacted excessively to any emotional stimulus. He needed supervision to protect him from society.

Stuart had a similar injury to the right frontal lobe of his brain following a car accident. The damage he suffered destroyed part of his emotional system and he was left without feelings. He had difficulty getting up in the morning, lacked motivation and enthusiasm, didn't use emotional words, and showed no signs of emotion. He felt indifference to everybody and everything.

The Biological Function of Emotions

In his book *The Feeling Of What Happens*, Antonio Damasio claims that the biological function of emotion is twofold.

The first function is to produce a specific reaction to a stimulus. For example, if an animal is threatened, the emotional response of fight, flight or freeze enables it to survive. In humans this basic mechanism may still function, but it is tempered with logic and wisdom.

The second function is to regulate the mind/body complex so that it can be prepared for reaction. In order to have the action of fight, flight or freeze, for example, there must be chemical, nervous and muscular changes. These basic changes represent the second part of the biological function of emotion.

It follows that emotions are essential rather than luxury aspects of human beings. They help to keep in balance events as diverse as reproduction or impending death.

Learning to handle emotions is essential for a cohesive society. If feelings get out of control, relationships are shattered and achievements fail to materialise. Having emotions as servant or partner rather than a master means that a symbiosis is occurring, where the whole is greater than the parts.

Treat your emotions as a servant or partner rather than a master.

Emotion and Motivation

Both 'motivate' and 'emotion' derive from *movere*, the Latin for 'to move'. Their relationship is further reinforced by the fact that emotions play a major role in motivating us to do what we wish or need to do.

When motivation and energy are lacking we're quite likely to say, 'I don't *feel* like doing that.' When motivation and energy are very high, on the other hand, we move easily towards our objective, and this is called the 'flow state'. Sportsmen and successful businessmen often report being in this state when competing or completing a deal. They comment that 'things just seem to be achieved without any effort'.

Motivation is closely intertwined with emotion, acting as a general energiser. This means that when we are in an emotional state, either high or low, our energy is vastly altered, increasing with joy or decreasing with sadness.

Emotions and Attention

Aristotle said, 'Feelings are conditions that cause us to change our judgements.' This is another way of describing the relationship between the head and the heart. When we pay attention to something we are focusing on it, thinking about it, judging it and considering how it relates to our situation. Emotion could be described as a spotlight focusing on our thoughts, attitudes and activities.

For most of the time this 'attention spotlight' is unfocused, illuminating a large area with less light because we are in a relaxed state thinking about a variety of subjects. When we have an emotion the spotlight contracts, throwing more intense light onto a smaller area. The emotion is directing our attention to a specific thought or object. For example, if we are afraid, we focus intently on what frightens us; when we are jealous the spotlight distracts us away from anything except the person we are jealous of; when we feel shy our attention is aimed solely at fading into the background.

Emotions and Memory

Memory has three components – input, storage and retrieval. Every day we receive millions of pieces of information through our senses, but we remember only a very small proportion of them. The situation at the time of input is vital in determining our ability to recall particular information.

Emotions have a major impact on the effectiveness of input and storage, while moods are important at the time of retrieval. Research has demonstrated that an emotional event is more easily recalled than a neutral one. When a powerful emotion occurs it heightens the senses, enabling the input and storage to be more efficient.

Sometimes input is distorted by emotions, and the memory process creates an inaccurate recording. The bias of this process depends on what form of emotion is present at the input stage. A relaxed environment at the time of input will distort the retrieval in favour of recalling happier aspects of the event. If anxiety is the dominant emotion, the components recalled will tend to be of a frightening nature.

Case History

Jonathan suffered from cancer and had received treatment in the form of surgery, radiotherapy and chemotherapy.

During his first course of treatment he had been so violently ill that the oncologist was concerned that he might not be able to complete a second three-month course. He referred Jonathan to me for help to reduce his nausea and vomiting while chemotherapy was being administered.

Jonathan told me that his experiences with doctors, hospitals and treatment had flooded him with fear, sadness, anger,

hopelessness and helplessness. When these feelings overwhelmed him, he believed that his body caused the vomiting
in order to reject what was making him feel so bad.

We discussed the fact that the drugs were targeted at his
cancer and trying to help him rather than hurt him. We
formulated a plan whereby any sensory stimuli he received
when he went to hospital (sights, sounds, smells, etc.) would
be reframed as helpful rather than terrifying. He learnt a self-
hypnosis technique to relax and 'escape' to a holiday resort
while the drugs were helping him, and to use his calmness to
allow his body to work normally.

In effect Jonathan was re-training his emotional memory, altering the perspective he had acquired from his previous hospital
experience, to one where hospitals were good rather than bad. So
successful was this strategy that he was able to have his
chemotherapy with minimal side-effects, and he continued to
keep his new perspective and emotional memory for the
remainder of his treatment.

Emotions and Judgement

Moods and emotions play a major role in the way we judge
people and events. When in a happy mood we reflect on good
things happening to us; when in an anxious mood we notice
worrying things around us, such as floods and famine. Our
emotions are not only guiding the way we see things, but they
also help determine the things we see.

The process of making judgements is, in theory, a rational
one, involving logical processes and incorporating all the available information to achieve the best outcome. Often, however,
emotions intrude upon the process, colouring it favourably or
unfavourably. When emotion takes hold it is very difficult to
prise it away with logical arguments.

Assessing people's character, however, is more accurately

performed using the emotional rather than the rational system. Deciding whether or not to trust someone relies more on emotion and intuition than logic. Those deficient in emotional skills have much greater difficulty in judging someone's character than those using gut reactions.

Emotions and Persuasion

In order to convert someone to our way of thinking we can use rational or emotional arguments. In many cases, the emotional appeal is much more successful, but be aware that its extreme form is emotional blackmail (see chapter 14).

Being open to the emotional influence of others makes us vulnerable, which can be frightening to those who lack confidence. By definition, vulnerability means 'exposed to damage or temptation' and implies that harm may follow. For those who are confident, vulnerability holds no fear as they are able to protect their 'openness'.

'Playing to the emotions' is a very powerful way of influencing someone. Declaring, 'You will feel so much better if you do this' is likely to be more effective than providing factual information to illustrate your point of view. For example, more people become vegetarian for sentimental reasons about killing animals than for practical reasons related to using land for crops rather than grazing.

The advertising industry uses emotive pictures, captions and subject matter to make an impact. Although the impact may be beyond our logical thinking, we are persuaded to buy the product because our emotions are leading us to do so: there is no interference from our analysing, questioning mind.

Emotions and Relationships

In 1759 a philosopher named Adam Smith stated: 'Emotions are the thread that weaves together the fabric of society.' With this he provides a very powerful answer to the question of why we have emotions.

Emotions are at the core of every relationship. While it is possible to have a relationship without feelings, it would be very distant, colourless and cold. We relate and communicate through our feelings; we judge a relationship by the emotional intensity it possesses; we value our relationships according to the variety of feelings engendered by them.

Among the emotions we might expect to feel are love, closeness, tenderness and trust. But perhaps the most important emotion is empathy (see chapter 8), the power to recognise the feelings of others. Without empathy, relationships crumble due to the lack of understanding and communication. The fellow feeling between two people is a much more powerful connection than any shared rational beliefs.

Parenting involves empathy – nurturing the emotional needs of the child with feelings such as love, happiness and support. When the child feels he is wanted, understood, needed, respected and loved, a strong foundation is being built to support a future adult. Giving and receiving love is the hallmark of a close family: the absence of these things creates a distant one.

Some people, such as egocentrics and psychopaths, are unable or choose not to have empathy. So consumed are they by their own needs that they are unaware of the feelings of others.

There are also those whose emotions were distorted by bad parenting so their capacity for empathy is greatly reduced. This can wreak havoc with their relationships.

Relationships are woven together by emotion. Intimacy can only occur when emotional secrets are shared and trust allowed to grow. Vulnerability – the baring of one's soul – is necessary when emotions are shared; fear of vulnerability creates distance. As relationships are the basis for propagation of the species, and propagation is necessary for survival, need we look any further for the answer to the question 'Why do we have emotions?'

3

Personality Types

'I recognise that I am made up of several persons and that
the person who at the moment has the upper hand will
inevitably give place to another.'

W. SOMERSET MAUGHAM

This chapter looks at eight different personality types and reveals
some fascinating facts – not least how personality determines
the way we use and are used by our emotions.

Some years ago when I was running a seminar for a group
of hypnotherapists, I asked for a volunteer to come to the front
so that I could demonstrate a psychological technique. A woman
ventured forward to sit on the chair next to me.

I talked to her for some time and asked about the conflicts
in her life. At one stage we touched on a sad incident and she
started to sob. I let her cry, supporting her as she explored the
emotions relating to her experiences. All of a sudden another
woman in the group ran up to the sobbing volunteer and started
drying her tears with a tissue.

'You monster!' she shouted at me. 'How could you just sit
there and watch her suffer?' I was taken aback by this outburst
and stunned into silence. After a little while the volunteer calmed
down and the irate woman left the seminar in high dudgeon,
uttering comments such as, 'I can't imagine how he ever became
a therapist. He is an uncaring beast!'

At the coffee break I sought out the volunteer to apologise
for my behaviour. She said she had been feeling perfectly well,

involved in her thoughts and feelings, and beginning to understand her sorrow, when she was interrupted by the other woman trying to fix her.

Looking back at that incident, I realise that the three people involved had different emotional responses, just as witnesses to an accident will recall it in completely different ways.

My attitude was that of a teacher helping the volunteer (and group) to learn about emotions and how to deal with them. I saw my role as being dispassionate, non-intrusive and supporting. I felt comfortable allowing the volunteer to discover what she needed to learn about her feelings, even if she was sad in the process. I saw the tears as an indication of her emotional state, not something to fix.

I believe that the angry woman who rushed out was feeling pain on behalf of the volunteer. She saw the tears as a sign of despair and grief requiring a remedy. Her view of me, as an observer, was expressed forcibly because of the angry emotions welling up inside her. She was a 'fixer' and saw 'acceptors' like me in a very poor light. Her role was to extinguish 'pain' wherever she found it.

The volunteer stated that she felt okay with her discomfort, and supported in her exploration. She had volunteered for a specific purpose – to learn about herself – and didn't want 'fixing'. Her tears were a sign that her journey was taking her into sadness that she hoped would lead to understanding and resolution. The emotions were within her acceptable limits, and she realised that the group and I were supporting her as she ventured along that road.

The three principal characters involved in this incident had unique emotional personalities that dictated their attitudes and actions. Each of us belonged to one of eight distinct personality types.

When a white light is shone through a prism it is refracted into the colours of the rainbow – red, orange, yellow, green, blue, indigo and violet. The warm colours (red shades) appear at one end, the cooler ones (blue shades) at the other. The middle colour (green) is a combination of warm (yellow) and cool (blue).

Emotional personalities may be graded in a similar manner. Those whose attitudes are dominated by emotion are at the red end of the spectrum, others whose lives are ruled by logic are at the violet end. In the middle are the balanced green ones.

People ruled by the heart are driven by feelings. That is how they know who they are and where they are going. For them feelings act as a compass, providing a certainty of response to any situation. Feelings determine their reaction to the outside world, just as a bats' echo-sounding interprets obstacles encountered during flight.

Those at the violet end of the spectrum are more cerebral – reason is king. They bring intellect to bear in all encounters. Emotions are unrecognised or undervalued, seen as distortions of the rational truth. Such people use logic to make sense of the world and have trouble in relationships, where emotion is queen.

Those in the centre, of greenish hue, are blessed with the ability to recognise the benefits of both ends of the spectrum, just as an artist makes use of all the colours in his palette.

Personality Types

Emotional differences between men and women are the subject of many books, theories and discussions. The difference between their attitudes, valuation and use of emotions can cause confusion and difficulties in relationships.

Women value feelings, express them and seek them in others. They regard them as the currency of relationships, and the need to share and discuss them is paramount. Feelings, they believe, are gold to the silver of rationality, so why do men value this silver so highly?

'I tell him how I feel and he completely ignores me. He drones on about points of view and logic until I'm completely bewildered and wish I'd never started the discussion in the first place.'

'When I tell him how I'm feeling, he looks at me blankly and goes back to reading the paper.'

'He is always talking facts, reason, outcomes. He never talks about himself and how he feels. I know he is more intelligent than I am, but when I ask about his feelings I end up feeling inferior and stupid.'

I regularly hear such comments from female clients when talking about their partners. They are disappointed, bewildered and unfulfilled by the emotional chasm that separates them.

On the other hand, men complain:

'My wife is always prattling about how she feels. She spends an hour on the phone talking to friends about nothing at all.'

'I can never get any sense out of my wife. She is always talking about how she and everyone else feels. She takes no notice of anything I say about the business, finance or what is happening in the world.'

In his bestselling book *Men Are from Mars, Women Are from Venus* John Gray discusses emotion from a variety of viewpoints, and lists the emotional needs of men and women:

Men need from their partners	Women need from their partners
Trust	Caring
Acceptance	Understanding
Appreciation	Respect
Admiration	Devotion
Approval	Validation
Encouragement	Reassurance

Difficulties arise because we tend to give what we want to receive. As the two lists show, what we give is not necessarily what our partner wishes to receive, hence the confusion and misunderstanding. By learning what your partner wants you are in a much better position to give it, with resulting harmony.

In the text that follows the eight basic personality types are described in simplified terms. As you probably know from your own experience, life isn't simple, and people rarely fit neatly into one category. As you read about these personalities, think about yourself, or others who may demonstrate some of the behavioural patterns. Each type has its benefits and drawbacks.

The cold fish

Those who display no emotion are called alexithymic, a term deriving from the Greek, meaning 'lacking words for emotion'. People described as such may have feelings but be unable to express them, or may lack the ability to feel. The cause of such a personality is unknown. Suggestions have been made that it stems from parents who were unemotional, or who failed to respond to the emotional needs of their child; emotional capability may have been reduced as the child learnt to respond with the mind rather than the heart.

Alexithymics lack the full spectrum of colours and rely on the ice blue of reason to deal with the world. In this they have no choice, and are misunderstood by those who cannot comprehend their lack of emotion. Much of life is bewildering to them as they have no access to emotional responses and have difficulty making sense of others who do.

Not only are they unaware of their *own* feelings, but they also lack the ability to notice emotions in others. This means that empathy is a closed book to them, so they have great difficulty in relationships. It is as if the two partners are speaking a different language, and neither knows how to translate the other's vocabulary. It is no wonder that confusion, anger and frustration result.

When you meet alexithymics (generally men) they have a flattening effect, talk in factual terms, use unemotional words, such as 'interesting', and steer clear of any discussions involving feelings. They relate only to reality, facts and experiences recounted at an intellectual level.

The partners of alexithymics are often at their wits' end. As emotions are a major currency for women, they want to know how their partner feels, but if he himself is unaware of this, he will obviously be unable to convey it to anyone else. The more the wife seeks an answer, the more withdrawn the husband becomes. Arguments ensue, and miscommunication and misunderstandings add fuel to the fire. Either the wife seeks help in therapy or sends her husband to be 'fixed'.

The cold inner world of the alexithymic is grey and colourless compared to the vibrant world of emotional people. He has trouble with fantasy because reality is his yardstick. His is the world of a deaf person trying to describe a symphony, or a blind person attempting to eulogise about the glowing colours of a sunset.

Life for the alexithymic could be described as a veneer. Whereas others plunge into the depths of their emotional world, he is forced to skim the surface of rationality. While he has the advantage of not being blown off course by intense and inappropriate emotions that cause problems for so many people, he misses out on the troughs and crests that colour life.

Case History

Daniel was married with three teenage children. His own father was an alcoholic and had used his emotions as a battering ram to upset and manipulate him. In order to survive childhood, Daniel shut off his own feelings and stopped saying what he felt because it only caused him trouble and pain. Instead, he avoided emotions at all costs and focused entirely on his rational mind.

So Daniel 'stayed in his head' and performed well academically. He became a teacher and was very competent at imparting his knowledge to the students; but something was lacking, and this caused difficulties with his wife, children and pupils. He was seen to be 'different', distant and unable to create warmth in the family. Daniel's children suffered because of this lack of warmth: they went off the rails, becoming aggressive and unruly. His wife tried to deal with the household but became depressed and withdrawn by the effort.

When Daniel consulted me he spoke vehemently about emotions being 'the enemy, used for manipulation, causing a loss of control, of no value'. He respected only facts, logic, reason and proof. He understood criticism but praise was completely foreign to him: it was a trap that could be used to control and manipulate him.

Daniel had indoctrinated his children with his beliefs and was just beginning to realise the damage it had caused. He was bewildered by our discussions and constantly retreated into his rational side to avoid the terrible pain of vulnerability.

Daniel illustrates the damage that can be caused when emotions are absent from relationships. Just as eating paper provides no flavour or nourishment, so relationships without emotion are no relationship at all. The lack of warmth in Daniel's family and work situations eroded all the benefits instilled by reason.

Partial blockers

Some people are able to partially block out feelings. Their mind is elsewhere, but their body shows appropriate emotional responses to whatever is happening. It is as if emotion is occurring in the system, but it is protected from the conscious mind at the same time as being received by the body.

Such a person may be in a situation where their body is showing all the signs of anxiety – racing pulse, sweaty palms and raised blood pressure – but when asked how they feel their reply is 'Completely calm'. It is not as if they are denying or lying about the situation, because studies of brain patterns show that they actually *are* feeling calm. The neural pathways in their brain divert the anxiety-inducing information away from conscious thought so that while the body is acting appropriately, the mind remains calm and relaxed.

This unawareness also occurs in extreme situations, such as intense warfare, where a soldier may be so intently focused on protecting his life that he is unaware of his emotions until safely away from the conflict.

An interesting hypnotic experiment sheds some light on this phenomenon. A research professor in the USA was exploring the ability to create analgesia (pain relief) through hypnosis. To do so a volunteer held his arm in ice-cold water until the pain was so great that he had to remove it. The time taken for this to occur was noted.

The volunteer was then hypnotised, it was suggested that he would feel numbness and no pain, and the arm was again placed in the iced water. This time he could hold it longer in the water before removing it due to pain. When asked about the feeling he had while his arm was immersed in the water, he stated that he felt no pain.

One subject went very deeply into hypnosis and during the second part of the experiment, after commenting that he felt no pain, another voice inside him called out that it was very painful. The professor doing the experiment got quite a shock on hearing this and repeated the experiment with other subjects, only to find the same outcome. He postulated the concept of a 'hidden observer' – part of the unconscious mind that is always aware even though other parts of the mind are asleep or anaesthetised. Further studies of recall during operations have arrived at the same conclusion. People who are partial blockers may be using this mechanism to deal with difficult situations, the body being the 'hidden observer' demonstrating feelings that are blocked from the conscious mind.

Emotional vampires

One of the aims in life is to learn to like and accept ourselves. Giving ourselves love charges our batteries, enabling us to deal with life's ups and downs. If we lack self-love because of bad parenting, childhood experiences or modelling on unemotional parents, we are deficient in an essential ingredient of life: our self-love container is depleted. Just as a car needs petrol in the tank for a journey, so we need self-love to see us through the day.

If we are deficient in self-love we seek the second-best option – love, praise and recognition from others. Emotional vampires, as I call them, depend on energy from others to survive. Because of their low self-worth they need to siphon praise and attention from other people in order to feel better about themselves.

Just as a car needs petrol for a journey so we need self-love to see us through the day.

Such people are needy, focused on themselves and very concerned about what others think of them. They constantly divert conversation towards themselves, their opinions, activities or needs. Those associated with them go away feeling drained and unfulfilled as their own needs are not being met. The energy gained by the emotional vampire from such transactions is short-lived: it is as if the petrol of external praise is merely two-star, while self-praise is four-star, providing more energy and lasting longer.

Emotional vampires are sad figures as they can never get enough. When told they are wonderful, their face may beam, but it is only a matter of hours till reassurance is required again. Those who take on the task of supplying their needs end up exhausted and disillusioned.

An emotional vampire may be compared to a compulsive gambler who craves the excitement of gambling to survive. After losing all his money, he borrows from family and friends. When this supply dries up, leaving angry and unhappy people in his wake, he moves to illegal methods to satisfy his craving.

The emotional vampire will not be 'fixed' by being given more attention and praise. He needs to realise that the answer lies within himself – self-praise, acceptance and a build-up of self-esteem.

Balanced personalities

People who seem well-balanced have an emotion/logic ratio that draws on both ends of the personality spectrum. The warm yellow and cold blue combine to form balanced green. Having access to both rationality and emotion means that many choices are available – you can respond to circumstances in a variety of ways.

Balanced personalities have a constant communication between head and heart so that appropriate and up-to-date responses occur. Such people are generally calm and confident, able to be emotional when the situation requires, and to apply rationality when that is most suitable.

If you feel you don't fit into this category but would like to, take heart – it *is* possible to change and learn new behaviours.

Disconnected personalities

People who have access to both logic and emotion but apply them independently of each other can be described as disconnected personalities. Most of us suffer from this occasionally. The head is unaware of the heart, and difficulties arise in decision-making when both power sources are sending contradictory messages at the same time. For example: 'I love her but can't live with her.' Or 'I know it's stupid but I feel terror at the sight of a mouse'.

Disconnected people are often in conflict: they receive messages to go left and right concurrently, and become confused and despairing as a result. Generally, past experiences have derailed the connection between rationality and emotion. An aeroplane flight with turbulence may set off an emotional response designed for survival, giving rise to the thought, 'Don't fly or you will die'. The logical mind is aware of the statistics proving that flying is safe, so the hapless victim of these two directives is caught in a tug of war.

This state of affairs generally occurs in specific situations rather than as an overall policy – indeed, most of us have experienced it from time to time – but some people are constantly caught in the battle between head and heart.

Emotionally unstable personalities

People who are run by their emotions are driven by the red end of the scale: logic comes a poor second in any internal discussion. Passion is the god and rationality has no value and little influence. The inner world of emotionally unstable people is either a swirl of vibrant colours or completely black. They could be described as 'all over the place'.

An extreme example is the condition called bipolar affective disorder, previously known as manic depression. In such cases the mood may be extremely high (manic) for days or weeks, with bouts of optimism, irrationality or recklessness. This is followed by a plunge into depression, characterised by bouts of negativity and hopelessness. The condition can be stabilised with prescription drugs.

The most common form of emotional instability is seen in those whose lives are dominated by feelings. Logic is absent and extremes are the norm. Typical is the 'crisis queen', for whom every situation is a drama. Such characters fluctuate from peaks to troughs, barely noticing the calm, flat state in between. The energy they radiate, whether positive or negative, is overwhelming, and their take on life is often far from the truth. Like a boat buffeted by winds from all directions, they lack the stability of a rational rudder.

Passionate personalities

The passionate person is at the opposite end of the spectrum from the alexithymic. She (they are generally women) has powerful emotions driving her from within, and values them above all else as the currency of life.

Relationships, excitement and creativity are what matter – facts and figures are too cold and calculating for her approbation. She loves life with a fervour and is enthusiastic about all her passions.

The strength of her feelings sometimes leads her astray, enveloping her in an inappropriate emotion. In these situations she loses control as the emotion is too powerful for her to have contact with reason. At these times she may need help from friends or therapists to rescue her from the powerful feelings driving her off course.

When feelings run our lives and drive us away from the shore of rationality we add another emotion – fear. The feeling of being out of control is not a pleasant one, and the thrill of passion is often negated by the flood of emotion it brings.

Passionate people require passion in their partners. Relationships may be fiery but they are never boring. To such people the cool customer is like a figure from another planet, a two-toed sloth to the howling baboon – misunderstood and undervalued.

Single-emotion personalities

Some people have access to the whole range of emotions, others do not: their lives are dominated by one colour in the spectrum – perhaps the vivid crimson of anger. Such people respond to life events as if their internal canvas is totally covered in red, causing them to react to any conflict with rage and fury. Others may have the ice-blue canvas of fear dominating their inner world, limiting access to the warm colours of safety and security.

Case History

Bill glows with anger. He has a long history of arguments and aggression. He sees the world in such a way that disagreements cause a volcano to erupt inside him. He is blocked from his understanding and compassion, doesn't give people the benefit of the doubt, and sees things in black and white (actually red) – they are wrong and he is right. This attitude causes him to lash out verbally or physically.

He sought help after realising that things were going from bad to worse when he punched a parking attendant and was faced with a court appearance. 'It happens all the time: I see something or someone says something, I feel myself getting hot with anger and explode. I know it's stupid but I just can't control it. When I cool down I realise what an idiot I've been, but by then the damage has been done.'

Bill had developed this response from a lifelong association with anger. It was the currency in his household when he grew up. He found it gave him dominance at school, and when he went to work as a builder he noticed the respect others gave him if he threw his weight around.

The therapy Bill needed was to learn about other emotions more appropriate to the situation and find ways to connect to them before his hair-trigger anger exploded.

Seeing Other Points of View

One of the benefits of dividing personalities into categories is to see how life is experienced by different individuals. Just because you think and feel in a certain way about an event does not mean that others will react similarly, but this can be hard to assimilate. Let's look at a situation from the perspective of each personality type outlined earlier. Imagine that a partner arrives home late on a night when there is an important dinner engagement.

- The alexithymic may calculate the effect of the time lost and call the people involved to explain the delay.
- The partial blocker may appear calm and unflappable, but generate bodily signs of annoyance and concern.
- The emotional vampire may require apologies and reassurances that the tardiness is not a sign that she is at fault.
- The balanced personality would combine concern about the lateness with rational reasoning that it was unavoidable, and deal with it in a manner that causes minimal fuss.
- The disconnected personality would be torn between imagining the latecomer in a traffic jam or car crash and feeling angry at their lateness.
- The emotionally unstable person may be all over the place, suffering a range of emotions from anger to guilt. A scene would occur and the late partner would be harangued all the way to the dinner.
- The passionate personality may be overcome by emotion, imagining that the hostess will be distraught by their late arrival. Her anxiety and concern may overwhelm her if she is out of touch with reason.
- The single-emotion personality may respond by punching the wall or his partner, and accompany these actions with a torrent of abuse. The drive to the dinner would be like an electrical storm, and the evening would be ruined for his partner by the resulting fear and guilt.

We are what we are. Recognising this fact, and being aware of the influence our feelings have on our view of the world, is an important first step towards making an improvement to the colours of our emotional palette.

4

Achieving Harmony between Reason and Emotion

'The heart has its reasons of which reason knows nothing.'
BLAISE PASCAL

This chapter examines the two forces that drive us – thoughts and emotions – and looks at the ways they can be helped to work in unison and bring harmony to our life.

An intrinsic aspect of a work of art is harmony – the way perspective, colour and composition work together to achieve balance. With humans, harmony is achieved when the mind/body system is in balance.

The most common cause of imbalance is when different parts of our make-up exert an excessive or deficient influence. For example, caution can be a useful quality, providing us with a basis for control, but if it grows to excess, it becomes anxiety, making us lose control and become dominated by fear.

Reason and emotion are two of the main influences on our character. When they are in harmony life is relatively easy; when at odds with each other life can be a struggle. Internal conflicts can be just as demanding as those we face in the external world.

You may say, 'I know all this but how can I do anything about it? I know my feelings are not in tune with my thoughts but just knowing this doesn't help to resolve the situation.'

Knowing is, in fact, an essential step towards finding a solution. Being aware or bringing conscious awareness to a situation indicates that we are gaining control and acquiring choices. This is an important step in integrating the various components of the mind/body system.

The intellectual and emotional components act in different parts of the mind/body system. Being focused on one does not necessarily help us with the other. As emotions are not always logical (they have a mind of their own), they are not understood if we remain in the rational state. There is an emotional logic to our feelings but it often differs enormously from our rational logic.

'I am terrified of travelling on the tube' is a statement of emotional logic that may arise from the following thoughts:

> 'I need to be in control.'
> 'When the doors close I can't get out.'
> 'What if I have to get out and I can't?'
> 'I will therefore avoid the tube at all costs.'

Rational logic applied to this problem would be:

> 'Millions of people travel on the tube and are safe.'
> 'I won't need to get out in a hurry.'
> 'If I need to get out, I will wait until the next stop.'
> 'It is therefore fine for me to travel on the tube.'

These two forms of logic are quite different and lead to completely opposite outcomes. Emotional logic is created by past experiences, stored emotions, survival mechanisms, the mood at the time and the need for control, and exerts its influence via bodily sensations, such as feelings of panic.

Rational logic involves thoughts occurring in a linear fashion, A leading to B leading to C. This process is reinforced by experience, as follows:

> 'I believe it is safe to travel on the tube.'
> 'I travel on the tube and it is safe.'
> 'My belief is reinforced and applied to future journeys.'

Emotional logic is not influenced by experience. Excuses masked as reasons maintain the original attitude in spite of experiences to the contrary.

Case History

Amy was frightened of travelling by bus, especially buses where the doors were closed while the bus was in motion. I used a number of techniques to lessen her fear and she agreed to travel on a bus for one stop and be aware of her response. At the next consultation she related that she had travelled ten stops without any fear.

'I suppose you feel much better now after that successful experience?' I ventured.

'Not at all,' she replied, 'the bus journey was on a Sunday and that doesn't count!'

Reconciling Two Types of Logic

Emotional logic and rational logic provide us with ways to understand and cope with the world. Both are valuable, and only cause problems when they are inappropriate, out of date or disconnected. Just as we have two hands that we can use individually or in partnership, so it is with reason and emotion. It is important to use whatever is most appropriate for the situation.

Too often emotion enters the territory of logic and causes confusion and conflict: 'When my son discusses his financial situation, my husband gets furious and adds fear to the negotiations. My son then becomes reticent and sullen and nothing is resolved.'

The discussion about the financial situation has a basis in rationality – the father wants to know about the money the son has available, so talking about money is appropriate.

However, there are emotional aspects relating to past experiences between father and son, so emotion breaks through and distorts the discussion, preventing resolution.

If the conversation could occur on two separate fronts, the logical monetary one and the emotional one relating to past experiences, perhaps both could move towards resolution.

Sometimes it is difficult to distinguish thoughts from feelings. We know we have an attitude about something but may not be sure if we are feeling it or thinking it.

A feeling is a one-word description incorporated in a sentence such as, 'I feel angry'. The direction of the sentence is towards yourself as you are the one with the feeling.

If you say, 'I feel that he is angry with me,' this is a thought because you are commenting on someone else, not yourself, so a more accurate sentence might be: 'I believe he is angry with me because I am feeling scared.'

One of the reasons we have difficulty achieving harmony between reason and emotion is that they have different ways of processing information. In order to understand these processes it is helpful to think of an emotional mind and a logical mind.

The emotional mind processes information quicker than the rational one, and mistakes happen because this speed often causes false recognition. First impressions start the sequence of events, which move so rapidly that they are untouched by reason. It is as if our 'emotional radar' focuses on highlights and loses sight of balancing factors. This is an evolutionary process to protect us from predators, but it may be an inappropriate response in 21st-century life.

A woman lying in bed at night, on her own while her husband is away, might scream if a moth flies near her. Her emotional radar is on full alert and the movement of the moth causes her emotional mind to process this event before her rational mind responds with a thought.

A second form of emotional reaction is slower and follows rational thought. We appraise a situation and emotions follow the appraisal: these emotions are balanced and helpful as they follow reflective thought. For example:

> 'My daughter isn't home yet and it's two a.m.' will lead to worry and concern.
> 'He promised to pay back the money he borrowed and that was two months ago' could lead to anger.

The fast type of emotion is thrust upon us before we can think. We do not choose it and are unable to use a logical process to decide if we wish to be taken over by it or not.

The emotional mind works by association and is triggered by the artistic language of music, poetry, metaphors, cinema and theatre. Anything is possible, and fantasy creates emotions that lie protected from logic. The emotional mind tends to stay fixed to its attitudes in spite of any logical representation that differs from them. It acts as if the present were the past because that is where the triggers originated (see chapter 10).

Three Steps to Mind/Body Balance

In order to benefit most from our thoughts and feelings we need the following:

1) appropriate messages from our emotions
2) rational thoughts
3) healthy interaction between thoughts and feelings

How can we achieve this state of affairs?

Step 1

We know when we are not receiving appropriate emotional messages – we feel out of control, uncomfortable, confused, limited, even that we may be going mad. Our feelings seem to have a mind of their own, driving us along detours and dead ends in spite of our knowing that something is amiss.

When a client visits a therapist the opening words are often, 'I know this is silly but I feel –'

This may be interpreted as: 'My rational mind knows this is silly but my emotional mind is in control and I feel –'

This illustrates the dichotomy that is constantly occurring in the mind/body system. In order to assist feelings to send appropriate messages we can use the following steps.

- Question the feeling and determine if it is helpful, suitable and up to date. Just as our senses of sight, hearing, taste, smell and touch inform us about the outside world and need to be accurate, so it is with emotions interpreting our internal world.

  A man who was constantly having car accidents had his eyes tested and discovered he was colour-blind. Instead of seeing red he saw green, so when the traffic lights directed him to stop, he accelerated, hence the accidents. In order to resolve his problem he needed to retrain his mind so that when he saw green it was actually red.

  So it is with emotions: we need to learn if the message we receive is accurate and suitable, otherwise we need to retrain our response so that a new feeling will grow. This retraining is not easy, as the pattern will have been laid down over many years, just as it was for the man who was colour-blind. Often people feel confused during this retraining state because their responses are very different to those they are accustomed to.

- The next step is to review the many times we have experienced feelings that were inaccurate and unhelpful. By spending quiet time reviewing these situations, we become aware of the misinformation we are continuously receiving from our emotions. In this way we begin to reprocess our responses by bringing to awareness the situation/feeling connections we wish to change.

- When the feeling recurs, stop and become aware of its presence and the effect it is having. Be determined that you will not let it continue to run/ruin your life. If the feeling directs you one way, go another – feel the fear and do it anyway. This attitude shows you are intent on wresting control from the emotion, allowing reason to have its influence.

- The last step is to replace the inappropriate feeling with one that is more in tune with your beliefs. Spend time deciding what you wish this feeling to be – calmness, confidence, safety or whatever. At regular intervals build up this new feeling so that it will be triggered by different situations. Gradually experience times when the previous feeling was triggered, stop and replace it with the new one. Use these situations, even if they are uncomfortable, as opportunities for improvement.

Case History

Leila was a 30-year-old mother of two who had been sexually assaulted by a neighbour when she was 13. Since that time she had been anxious and withdrawn, but her confidence had gradually improved following her marriage ten years before I saw her. She sought help to deal with an overwhelming fear when meeting new people. It was difficult for her to go to social occasions with her husband, and disagreements at home had caused her to seek my help.

Using the affect bridge technique (see chapter 24), we traced her fear back to the horrifying experience when she was 13. We then put the four steps discussed above into practice.

First Leila questioned whether the fear was suitable or helpful. She decided she would like to keep it as a protective device but at a lower intensity – 20 units instead of 100.

She then spent time reviewing experiences where she was frightened but the outcome was safe, all the times she felt something terrible would happen and it didn't. Her homework was to continue reprocessing this message and to keep a diary of her thoughts, memories and emotions that would provide evidence that her fear was unfounded.

Her next task was to stop herself when the fear occurred and take time to assess its validity. She challenged the fear and continued to do what she wanted in spite of its presence. In this way she was removing the reinforcing power maintaining her fear.

She also practised relaxation exercises to provide her with an alternative feeling to the fear, and used these exercises before she went to a social engagement. If necessary, she would slip out to the toilet and practise them again during a party. She worked hard at building up the feelings of calmness and security in order to introduce them when she was going out. Eventually, she was able to reduce the fear to a manageable level and include feelings of calmness and security.

Step 2

Now consider the second point: our thoughts need to be rational.

This might seem obvious, but all too often irrational thoughts trigger powerful, upsetting feelings. These are sometimes called automatic thoughts as they do not follow a reasoning process.

The psychological term for the thinking process is 'cognition', and a popular therapy exploring this process is called cognitive behavioural therapy. This utilises techniques and practical ways to assess thoughts and the outcomes that follow them. By improving our thinking processes, we can create more successful emotions, attitudes and behaviours.

Automatic thoughts stem from what is called a core belief deep in our unconscious. By asking suitable questions about our moods, responses and attitudes, we can uncover core beliefs that are often the basis of our difficulties. A core belief can be articulated in a short, succinct statement that is absolutist, inflexible and has unrestricted power.

'I am hopeless' is an example of a core belief. It is not qualified or lessened in any way, such as 'Sometimes I'm hopeless' or 'In certain situations I'm hopeless'.

Core beliefs focus on three things: me, other people and the world. Some common examples are:

- 'I'm unlovable.'
- 'I must please everyone.'
- 'Children should be seen and not heard.'
- 'Men are untrustworthy.'
- 'The world is a dangerous place.'
- 'India is full of sickness and poverty.'

These beliefs are imposed upon us by the brainwashing we received in childhood. If, when we made mistakes, we were repeatedly told, 'You did that because you are stupid,' over time we develop a core belief 'I am stupid,' which will influence the way we react to many situations. These core beliefs then create automatic thoughts, so it is important to become aware of their existence and change them to be more appropriate to the present attitude we have of ourselves.

Case History

Harry was a perfectionist and suffered the many problems that result from such an attitude. He was trying to fit the square peg of perfectionism into the round hole of life, and consulted me for symptoms of stress – panic attacks, sleep disturbance and hyperventilation. In the course of our consultation we explored ways to learn about his core beliefs, and discovered that one of them was, 'I have to be the best'. This belief had come about in his childhood, where in a family with three brothers and two sisters, he feared he would not be noticed unless he achieved more than the others.

His belief was enhanced by the attention he received when he *was* the best. Unfortunately, his core belief was now causing him problems, as he was using excessive energy in every aspect of his life and paid little attention to his own personal requirements. He often wanted to say no, but his perfectionism prevented him.

During the course of therapy, Harry altered his core belief to 'I need to be in balance', which respected his own needs and reduced the driving force that was previously in control. He learnt that he was being liked and respected for himself, and it was not necessary to perform continually as the best to receive recognition.

When we identify core beliefs, challenge them and improve them, we begin to relate to life as it actually is rather than how it has been imposed on us.

To learn about core beliefs we need to ask specific questions such as:

- What has caused me to think this way?
- Is there evidence to support that attitude?
- Did anyone in my past talk to me like that?
- What does that thought say about me or my view of the world?

It is important to alter core beliefs so that they are rational, up to date and can be verified by our experiences. If, for example, you believe 'The world is always against me', you need to ask yourself if there are any examples when this is *not* so. People often focus on their failures and ignore successes. By challenging core beliefs we achieve a more balanced attitude to ourselves, others or the world.

Some people are run by what are called 'non-disprovable theories'. This means that there is no way of disproving what they claim to be true. Look, for example, at the old belief in witches that was reinforced by using a ducking stool in the village pond. The rationale went as follows:

- Witches are evil and dangerous women.
- If you duck them in water and they survive, that proves they are witches, so they should be burnt at the stake.
- If they drown, that proves they are innocent.

Illogical though this is, many people hold beliefs that fit the same rationale. We (and they) cannot disprove what they are stating, so they hold onto the false logic, even though it leads them to an unhappy and unsuccessful life.

Case History

Joanne had been unhappily married for 20 years. She was subservient to her husband Peter, but resented the fact that he pushed her around. She cried as she discussed their relationship.

'He sits and watches TV while I run after his every need. I get no thanks or appreciation for all the things I do.'

'Why do you do them, then?' I asked.

'Because if I don't, he might leave me. My mother told me I always had to put my husband first, and that's what I do.'

Joanne was following a form of false logic that stated 'Wives must always be subservient to their husbands or the husbands will leave', although there was no evidence to support Joanne's belief. Peter had never threatened to leave if she didn't bring him dinner in front of the TV, but Joanne had been too frightened to challenge her mother's edicts.

During therapy she learnt that it was possible to be more assertive and still keep her marriage together. As she did more of the things that pleased her, she became a happier person, and Peter adapted to (and perhaps appreciated) the improvements that occurred in her behaviour.

Step 3

There needs to be a healthy connection between thoughts and feelings to enable them to interact with each other.

Often the difficulties people have are related not to thoughts or feelings, but to the connection between the two. The battle for control occurs at an unconscious level, and achieving harmony begins by being aware of all three – thoughts, feelings and connections.

'I think A but feel B' illustrates a lack of connection. The emotional force and rational mind are at loggerheads and unable to come to terms with each other.

'I know it's silly, but I'm terrified of mice' indicates a disparity between reason and emotion. By finding a way for logic to educate the feeling, we can achieve harmony and overcome the fear.

There are many techniques used to help reason and emotion work together. As they reside in different parts of the mind the connection needs to be achieved in a circuitous way. Directly challenging the feeling with logic is unlikely to make any improvement. Telling someone who's afraid of mice, 'Don't worry – they won't hurt you,' will be met with, 'I know that, but it doesn't help.'

The connection may be made with a practical experience in desensitisation, where a mouse is gradually brought closer to the person, but the person always remains in control. In this way we learn at a deeper level to let go of the fear, as our personal experience is showing us it is not necessary.

Cognitive behaviour therapy uses a series of challenging questions to create a connection between reason and emotion. Workbooks are used to chronicle daily experiences and then to question both the beliefs and emotions. At each review the client's personal events highlight any discrepancies between the two.

Visualisation (see chapter 24), is another technique that helps to show how connections may be absent or impracticable and how to develop new and more useful ones. This process uses the imagination to examine thoughts and feelings, and what is or isn't connecting them. It avoids logical constraints and uses the client's creativity to achieve success.

Case History

Roger's opening words were: 'I know it's ridiculous but I am so jealous of my partner Louise that she is threatening to leave unless I get help. She has never given me any reason to be jealous but I just can't help it. I'm swamped by it when I think she may be with other men.'

Roger and I talked about a number of different aspects of his situation. I learnt he had been bullied at school, had low self-esteem, and had experienced two relationships where his partners left him. Little wonder that he concluded he was unlikely to have a satisfactory long-term relationship.

He had developed a core belief of 'I am unlovable', and re-inforced that with the knowledge of his failed relationships. After much discussion, he decided that it would be feasible to change his core belief to 'I am lovable', with many examples to back it up. Later he agreed to learn about visualisation in order to alter his feelings of jealousy, so I helped him to relax, then asked him to imagine the thoughts in his mind. He imagined a typewriter printing messages. I then asked him to imagine his jealous feeling, and he immediately visualised a fiery ball in his stomach. The bigger the ball became, the more the jealousy intensified.

I then asked him to find the connection between the type-writer messages in his head and the fiery ball in his stomach. After some time he said he could see a ladder with many broken rungs. He saw this as completely inadequate to convey messages, so he decided to change it to a telephone line.

His homework was to spend time in a relaxed state using the telephone line to convey his new belief, 'I'm lovable', to the fiery ball in his stomach to influence or prevent the jealousy. Over the next few sessions he decided to have a tube carrying water as the connection so that the fire of jealousy would be doused by the 'I'm lovable' message in the water. He practised creating the feeling and then sending the message to remove it. He worked with Louise so that she became aware of what he was trying to do. When the jealousy started she would sit with him and help him douse the flames by supporting him with the words that she loved him and he was lovable.

In order to achieve harmony between our thoughts and feelings we need to have awareness about the messages we are receiving from both. As we learn about each component and the system connecting them, we can help them work together rather than pulling us in different directions.

5

Assessing, Protecting and Respecting Our Emotions

'Emotions are like children: they need care
and attention in many different ways.'

BRIAN ROET

Emotions do not exist in a vacuum – they affect every aspect of our lives, so it's a good idea to look after them. This chapter tells you how to do that, taking you through the processes of assessment, protection and respect.

Assessing Our Emotions

There are two broad categories of emotion: those that move us forward and those that hold us back. It is helpful to devote time and energy to learning about our feelings and asking ourselves which of these categories they fall into.

Think about the emotions you had yesterday, starting from when you woke up until you went to bed. Now ask yourself: 'Did my feelings move me forward or did they hold me back?'

For example: 'I arranged to have dinner with Sue at eight o'clock. She arrived at twenty past eight, and I felt embarrassed and foolish as I waited on my own in the restaurant. When she arrived I was so angry that the evening was ruined.'

Emotions are like children; they need care
and attention in so many ways.

The two emotions involved in this situation were embarrassment and anger. Having established that, the next step is to assess how they affected you.

'These two emotions held me back because they upset the evening and made me lose control of my communication with Sue. I would have preferred to be more understanding and kept it in proportion so I could have enjoyed Sue's company that night.'

By assessing our emotions we are not classing them as wrong or right, but as helpful or unhelpful. We can then think of feelings we would like to have in similar situations in the future. As our feelings are often powerful it is difficult to assess them in an unbiased way, with a calm mind and balanced attitude. Past experiences also may intrude, making it even more difficult to see things as they actually are and understand the other person's point of view.

Emotions that bind

One category of emotions that limits our choices I call emotions that bind. These are powerful feelings that occur in relation to a specific situation, person or subject, controlling the way we act and think. We become aware of such emotions when we realise they are occurring again and again, causing problems and preventing free will. We know of their existence when, for example, someone is 'on their hobby horse' and refusing to listen to any alternative opinion.

Case History

Trudy had an unpleasant mother, there is no doubt about that. She was critical, angry and overpowering.

'Whenever we meet she gives me a hard time, nothing I do is right and I leave feeling upset, angry and guilty.'

As we discussed her relationship it became obvious that Trudy was bound to her mother by five simple words, 'But she is my mother.'

These words created a feeling in Trudy that prevented her having any choice in the way she related to her mother. Any thought of answering back, being assertive, defending herself or separating were prevented by those five powerful words.

'How often do you have contact with your mother?' I asked.

Trudy's face grew hard and annoyed.

'I ring her every day and visit every second weekend. It used to be every weekend, but I couldn't cope with my children and housework as well, so after a lot of hassle and argument, she agreed to every second weekend.'

'Could you tell her how you feel and the effect she has with her criticism and judgement?'

At this point Trudy started sobbing.

'I would love to do that. I'm bursting to say something, but she's my mother and she would be so upset, so the words never come out of my mouth.'

> Trudy was bound (and gagged) by thoughts and emotions set in concrete that prevented her being herself with her mother. She was able to be assertive with friends, her husband and her children, but perhaps that was because 'They are not my mother'.

Emotions that bind are intense. They may be positive, like passion, love and joy, or negative, like jealousy, hate and fear. These intense emotions take us over and run the show; we are merely dragged along in their wake. Sometimes we may be so consumed by the feeling that we lose control and commit acts we later regret.

Binding emotions often have a hidden agenda. For example, explosive anger may be the result of low self-esteem. By exploring underlying factors we begin to understand the processes involved, and can restore balance and equilibrium to our emotional system.

At its most extreme, the binding nature of thoughts and feelings can cause some people to repeatedly follow a pattern of behaviour that will diminish unpleasant feelings that bind. This is called obsessive compulsive disorder, and my client Charlie was a prime example of it. In his case the hidden agenda was anxiety, demonstrated by his compulsive actions.

Case History

Charlie was travelling on a motorway and felt a bump as his car ran over something on the road. He thought 'Have I run over someone?'

He immediately became very anxious, so he left the motorway at the next junction and retraced his journey. When again on the motorway he slowed down at the place where he had felt the bump, and to his relief there was nothing on the road. As he continued driving another thought came into his head.

'What if you did hit someone and they have crawled into the bushes beside the motorway? What if they are lying there mortally injured?'

Once again anxious feelings overwhelmed Charlie, so he retraced his route, stopped his car on the hard shoulder and searched the bushes. Relieved to find nothing, he set off on his journey again, only to have another thought: 'What if the police found the injured person, have taken him to hospital and are looking for the culprit?'

In desperation he drove to the local hospital. It was only when he learnt no traffic accidents had occurred in the area that he was able to drive home without feeling anxious.

His emotions that bind had taken three hours to be subdued, and caused a great deal of pain and suffering in the process.

To understand more about binding emotions we need to ask ourselves: 'When we feel that way, do we have the freedom to assess the emotion, and does it fit in with our views and values, or is it in control and controlling?'

Intense feelings that take over often lead to ruminations – circular thoughts – and the binding is intensified. The mind becomes absorbed with the target of the emotion, and phrases such as 'if only', 'what if' and 'how could they' circulate in the mind, taking us further and further away from a balanced perspective.

Newspaper headlines often proclaim the actions of a lover whose passion has led to murder. The intensity of love is mirrored by the intensity of anger. Fury binds us to its breast, compelling us to perform acts completely against our nature. Our dark side takes hold when emotions that bind are in control. The stalker is tied to the victim by passion, the victim is tied to the stalker by fear.

Intense emotions need to be diluted in order to be servants rather than masters. The influence of reason (see chapter 4) plays a role in this balancing process.

Protecting Our Emotions

With feelings that bind we need to protect ourselves from our own emotions. At other times we need to protect them from outside interference. Like children, emotions are vulnerable, so our role as their guardian is very important.

Being vulnerable means being exposed, and our emotions *are* exposed to many external influences. In order to work in harmony with our feelings we need to look after them, respect them, value them and understand them. One way of achieving this is embodied in the Indian philosophy that regards emotions as sources of energy called *chakras*.

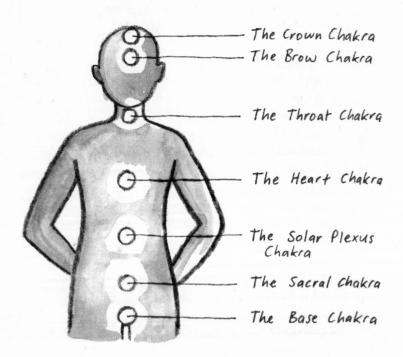

The Crown Chakra
The Brow Chakra
The Throat Chakra
The Heart Chakra
The Solar Plexus Chakra
The Sacral Chakra
The Base Chakra

The seven chakras are located in different sites in the body.

The protection of chakras

Chakra is the Sanskrit word for 'wheel', but in emotional terms a chakra is a concentration of energy situated in a specific part of the body. There are seven major chakras aligned along the vertical axis of the body. Each receives, stores and radiates energy relating to specific functions. When we interact with the external world, energy transfers occur through these chakras.

Chakras also store memories that are specific to their function. Becoming aware of chakras enables us to utilise them and open ourselves to outside influence, or to close them out, protecting ourselves from harmful intrusion.

The seven chakras

1 – located at the base of the spine, it governs physical constitution, sexuality and basic survival issues.

2 – situated in the pelvic area below the navel, it relates to emotional experiences, vulnerability and sharing.

3 – located in the solar plexus above the navel, it relates to the way we direct our emotional needs out into the world. It is a power centre where ideas are transformed into reality, and energy is created to express feelings and opinions.

4 – the heart chakra, in the centre of the chest, is the home of the soul and the centre for emotional expression.

5 – situated in the throat, it represents the conscious rational mind and governs speaking, listening, analysing and understanding.

6 – located behind the forehead, it relates to the unconscious mind, and is the site of imagination, belief systems and self-perception.

7 – the chakra of the spiritual self, is at the crown of the head. It radiates outwards, connecting to the outside world and nature. It also takes in energy from outside to complete the connection.

We can use chakras to help understand ourselves, our attitudes, beliefs, difficulties, the way we relate and where we are going. They interconnect to provide a basis for all our functions, representing the ways our emotions are affected by a variety of influences. Their energy can be described as free-flowing, out of balance or blocked.

The chakras themselves can be either open or closed, depending on the situation and our need for interaction or protection. Trudy, for example, was unable to close her chakras and protect herself against her mother's influence.

The main way we access our chakras and influence their activity is via meditation. The focus of the meditation is on a specific chakra to learn how it is functioning and assess if any adjustment is necessary. Some chakras (1, 3 and 5) are expressive, which means that the energy flows outwards. Other chakras (2, 4 and 6) are receptive, which means that the energy flows inwards. The seventh chakra flows in both directions.

For the mind/body system to be healthy, the energy needs to circulate freely so that harmony and balance exists between the chakras. When we suppress ideas, emotions or bodily needs, the energy slows and becomes stagnant. A variety of meditative procedures are available to rectify the situation and restore flow.

This brief discussion about chakras is aimed at helping you learn to protect your emotions from abuse or misuse. When you are open to someone, you are opening the receptive chakras and allowing outside influence to come in. This means you are vulnerable, so it is important to trust those around you at that time. Watch out for people who can harm you, such as the emotional vampire described in chapter 3.

Case History

Many years ago a friend asked if I would see his brother to help him stop smoking. I was pleased to be asked, and when the young man came to see me I tried very hard to be of assistance. To every suggestion he replied: 'I can't do that' or

'I'm not willing to try that', so after 20 minutes I told him I didn't think he was ready to stop just yet.

He became annoyed and commented that he had travelled some distance to see me, and believed I cured everyone. I told him this was not so, and he left in a bad mood. I was then taken by surprise as I could not get out of my chair: I felt completely exhausted, as if I'd run a marathon. It took me 10 minutes to function properly, and I went to my secretary to ask her opinion of the previous client.

'He was a terrible young man. He complained about every-thing – the chair, the decor, the fee, that he had to wait five minutes.'

I concluded from this episode that I had let down my defences, or opened my chakra to him, as he was the brother of a friend. Having lowered the protective mechanism that I usually have in place when meeting new clients, I was vulner-able to this extremely negative man, and he drained my energy to such an extent that I couldn't get out of my chair.

Because of this experience I realised I would need to protect myself against similar intrusions in the future. I now close my chakras when I am with clients until I feel safe with them and trust them enough to 'let them in'.

In order to protect your emotions it is very important to be aware – alert not only to outside influences, but also to internal feelings.

After my experience with the young man who drained my energy, I became aware of that potential in other clients too. When I first met them I kept a distance until I knew it was safe. This awareness has helped me to survive a long practice in psychotherapy. As I became more comfortable with a client, I gradually opened my chakras, knowing that it was safe to do so.

Many people have had their emotions trampled upon in child-hood, either at home or at school, and are reticent about re-experiencing that pain and humiliation. They become with-drawn and guarded, and close down all their chakras for protection. Helping such people to integrate and open up to the world is often a slow process. A rabbit that has been shot at and fears for its life is hardly likely to trust the person who puts a hand down its burrow and pulls it out by the ears to inform it that the hunters have gone.

So it is with emotionally harmed clients: they need to develop trust and feel safe at their own pace and in their own way. This allows them to protect their vulnerability until it feels comfortable to lower the barriers and relate to people without fear or concern.

I often ask clients to express their feelings in order to allow others to know where they are coming from. Their replies include:

> 'I can't. I'm too scared of how he might react.'
> 'I don't have the confidence to do that.'
> 'What will they think of me?'
> 'I don't want to be hurt again as I was with . . .'
> 'How do I know I can trust him?'
> 'I'd lose control if I did that.'
> 'He'd think I was strange for saying how I feel.'

Like so many other aspects of our mind/body system, expressing or protecting our emotions needs to be in balance. We need to recognise those situations where it is safe to allow our emotions out into the world, and be aware of those where protecting ourselves from hurt and disrespect is more appropriate.

The amount of emotional protection people need depends on their sensitivity, what might be called 'the thickness of their skin'. At one end of the scale those with thick skin can effec-tively protect their inner sanctum of emotions; at the other end, thin-skinned people are vulnerable and unable to defend them-selves against the onslaughts of the outside world.

There are benefits and disadvantages at both ends of the scale. Occupying the middle ground and having the ability to be vulnerable or protected allows the greatest flexibility in coping with whatever experience we encounter.

Respecting Our Emotions

During the course of my work I've found that many clients negate their feelings:

> 'I shouldn't feel that way.'
> 'Isn't it terrible to feel angry when he says those things about me?'
> 'It's so childish to cry over such a little thing.'
> 'I feel so guilty when I'm shy in company.'

Respecting the way we feel, even if it is not comfortable, allows us to learn more about our emotions and the messages they are attempting to express. Our feelings are our feelings – we cannot stop them occurring by denying or negating them. They may be unhelpful, out of date or holding us back, but by learning about them we can make changes.

By denying our unhelpful emotions we distance ourselves from them and give them more power. By respecting them, learning about them and updating them, we recover an asset that has gone astray due to previous trauma.

Our feelings are part of us; they need not overwhelm us and we need not overwhelm or deprecate them. We need to work in harmony with them, which requires two-way respect. We need to respect our feelings and our feelings should respect our needs.

When negotiation occurs between us and our feelings we arrive at a win/win situation, both working together for a common goal. As feelings have often been damaged and distorted by past experience, the negotiation needs to be gentle and respectful. Using a variety of techniques, such as visualisation, meditation, self-hypnosis, psychodrama and body work, we can get in touch with our feelings and allow two-way communication to occur.

As Aristotle said about anger, it is important to have emotions relating to the right person, to the right degree, at the right time and for the right reason. This chapter has set you on the path to achieving that.

6

Feedback Loops

'The feedback loop is to the body what the wheel is to transport.'
BRIAN ROET

Among the most important mechanisms in the mind/body complex are feedback loops, which help maintain balance or the status quo. They occur in every system of the body and mind, and use chemical and nervous transmission to maintain the internal environment within normal limits.

For example, a feedback loop exists between the blood sugar levels and insulin production. If the sugar level rises, so does insulin production, to maintain normal blood sugar levels. The reverse is true if the sugar level falls. If the body has a malfunctioning pancreas, as in diabetes, the feedback loop fails, so normality must be restored with artificial insulin administered by mouth or injection.

In a similar manner our eating pattern is controlled by a feedback loop which is automated by the level of nourishment in the blood and the appetite control centre in the brain.

Problems arise in the feedback loop when it is interfered with by external forces that make the balance different from the one nature intended. For example, if we were urged to eat every time we were upset, angry, sad, depressed, lonely or jealous – 'Have something to eat, dear, and you'll feel so much better' – an emotional factor would be introduced into the system. Instead of food being eaten for bodily requirements, it would become a 'fixer of negative emotions', distorting the loop to achieve a

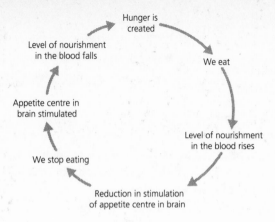

Food feedback loop

different aim – namely, make us feel better. The trigger to eat then comes to rely on a feeling rather than blood chemistry. Emotionally driven comfort-eating develops, and the food loop is now represented differently.

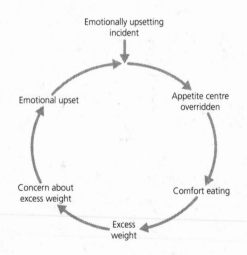

Comfort-eating feedback loop

There are a multitude of childhood messages that may distort the appetite control centre-blood chemistry eating loop:

'Finish everything on the plate.'

'Think of the people starving in India.'

'Eat up and you'll grow strong and healthy.'

'I didn't go to all the trouble of cooking for you to leave it on the plate.'

These words, and the action we take in response to them, override nature's feedback loop and replace it with one aimed at satisfying emotional needs. Of course, food will not resolve emotional problems – it just becomes a problem itself.

Feedback loops work with our emotions, just as they do with every other system in the mind/body complex. Our emotions, like our eating patterns, are to a large extent moulded by childhood experiences. If our emotions are abused in childhood, perhaps sensitivities and beliefs not respected, our emotional feedback system becomes distorted, maintaining avoidance and survival rather than exploration and growth.

Similarly, the belief that we are unlovable can lead to developing a feedback loop that maintains that belief. Any evidence to the contrary will be negated: if someone likes us, the loop suggests, that person must be of no value to like someone who is unlovable.

We can be aware when a negative feedback loop is working because we are constantly driven by our emotions towards attitudes and actions that are holding us back rather than moving us forward.

Case History

Phillip had suffered from panic attacks for five years. They were becoming more frequent and restricting his life. They occurred on the Underground originally, but had started to trouble him in other situations recently.

The feedback loop that was acting to maintain his fears could be stated as follows:

- Five years ago he had a panic attack on a Tube train. The

underlying cause (which was not addressed) was stress relating to his divorce, and overwork due to the expansion of his company.

- His thoughts and emotions focused on trying to avoid any further occurrences of panic, so he took tranquillisers and travelled by car.
- He developed the belief: 'Tube trains are not safe. I need to be in control.'
- Any news or reports of problems with the Tube reinforced his beliefs.
- Positive reinforcement came when he drove his car and felt in control.

Phillip's feedback loop

Phillip's feedback loop keeps him anxious and worried that he may have to travel on the Underground and he will have a panic attack. In fact, the attacks were occurring even though he wasn't travelling on the Tube. His panics were not related to the Underground, even though that's where he first encountered them: they were related to his stress and anxiety about his divorce and work.

By focusing on ways to reduce stress, relax and bring rationality into his thoughts, his panics subsided. He also learnt how to improve his breathing and reduce the hyperventilation that was playing a role in his problem.

Childhood emotions are like delicate seedlings, requiring nurturing and protection to grow into healthy, strong plants capable of withstanding nature's onslaughts and producing flowers and fruit. If they are neglected, mistreated or abused, their future potential is reduced, just as a gardener neglecting to water or nourish seedlings may expect to have a diminished crop.

The pool of emotions we store as adults reflects our childhood experiences. If we have received support, love and praise, the pool acts as a positive resource for future attitudes and beliefs. If we have received anger, blame and criticism, the pool will be diminished, and fear, guilt and anxiety added to contaminate it. The status quo established in childhood, whether good or bad, is the one that the feedback loop will maintain in adulthood, and it is very important to remember this.

Like a faulty compass, distorted feedback loops point us in the wrong direction and cannot be relied upon to guide us successfully through life. These malfunctioning loops give us incorrect information, create emotions inappropriate to the situation, and send us round and round in circles.

For example, someone terrified of flying will be unimpressed by statistics indicating that it is a very safe method of travel, and will use the emotional loop to distort the facts: 'I know it is 3 million to one that the plane will crash, but what if I am on *that* plane?' The energy of the loop is directed to maintain the status quo – 'I'm terrified of flying' – and seeks any way to achieve this, even by resorting to quasi-logical statements to defend the attitude held.

Recently, while on holiday in Thailand, I witnessed an unusual feedback loop working very successfully. While visiting a temple in the countryside I saw a woman with a number of cages containing small birds. She beckoned me over and indicated that for a small sum of money I could release the birds from the cage. This would bring me good luck and enhance my chances in the next life.

I paid the money, released the birds and felt my halo glow brighter. That night I was discussing the woman with a local resident and he smiled saying;

'Do you know what goes on behind the temple?'

'No,' I replied.

'Some little girls are there putting breadcrumbs on a table. When the birds are released they fly to the table, start eating and are put back in the cage to be returned to the woman.'

I expressed my indignation at such a corrupt scheme.

'She blackmailed me into paying money in the belief that I was freeing the birds and gaining my key to heaven, when they were just being recycled for her profit.'

'Not really,' my acquaintance replied. 'It's a cycle where everyone wins. You felt better for releasing the birds, she made some money, the little girls earned some money, and the birds were fed and had some freedom.'

It was indeed a successful feedback loop in every sense.

Changing Feedback Loops

How can we overcome factors that maintain inappropriate attitudes beliefs and feelings? The answer is not simple, even though some self-help books may imply that it is. The following points can help you to achieve your goal.

1. You must want to change. Motivation is the most important force for improvement.
2. Put in time and energy to overcome beliefs learnt in childhood. Approach this as a project that is important for your well-being.

3. Learn to be aware of your attitudes, beliefs and feelings.

4. Find someone to talk to – preferably a professional counsellor or therapist. Talking about your feelings will release them from the emotional pool and ensure that the feedback system isn't working on negative emotions.

5. Seek a technique, such as hypnosis or cognitive behaviour therapy, to correct distorted attitudes and thoughts.

6. Learn to overcome any powerful emotions that are limiting your choices by balancing them with rational attitudes.

7. Learn to be more confident, to say 'no', and to care less what people think.

8. When a challenge arises ask the question 'Why not?' to spur you on, rather than 'Why?' to maintain the status quo.

9. Make mistakes – they are the best way to learn anything new.

10. Develop the attitude 'What can I learn'? rather than 'Am I right or wrong?'.

11. Realise that there is no definite connection between feelings and actions. We can feel we should do A yet still do B.

12. Be aware of the 'child within' dictating behaviour with out-of-date feelings and internal messages.

13. Discover the components of your emotional feedback loops – the ones maintaining your difficulties. Create new components so that the loop promotes health rather than unhappiness.

14. Set aside theory in favour of experiences.

15. Find positive emotions to help you achieve your needs rather than focusing on the negative ones causing problems.

16. Remember that it takes time to change and that it's not always easy. Fix those things you can and accept those that you can't for the time being. Focus on the positive aspects of your day, give yourself praise and encouragement, and accept yourself as you are for now. This is the best springboard for improvement.

7

Body Language: Expressing Emotions Subconsciously

'It is slavery to live in the mind unless it
has become part of the body.'

KAHLIL GIBRAN

Like a ship's semaphore, the body continuously sends signals, conveying subtle and succinct messages for those able to read them. This chapter explores these secret signals and decodes the wealth of information they reveal about ourselves and others.

Recently I read a newspaper article about a dog called Sammy. He was a schnauzer and belonged to Jacqueline, a 45-year-old who suffered from severe epilepsy. Sammy was Jacqueline's 'early warning device'; his training enabled him to detect when she was about to have a fit even before she was aware it would happen. From minimal body cues, such as facial twitches and eye dilations, he could whine, bark or stare to let her know of the impending fit. Once alerted, Jacqueline could find a safe place to lie down and avoid injuring herself.

We all send subtle messages, cues and vibrations that are picked up by others, often beyond our conscious awareness. These vibrations are a reflection of our moods, and are detected on an emotional level rather than a logical one. This is illustrated by the story of clever Hans, a fine horse owned by a Prussian officer in the 19th century. Hans had achieved worldwide fame for his ability to do sums. His owner would hold up a board with a simple addition or multiplication sum and Hans would paw the ground a number of times to signify the answer.

Many scientists visited Hans to find out if the demonstration was a fraud, and came to the conclusion that it was not. Then a psychologist came to study Hans and asked if he, rather than the officer, could hold up the board showing the sum. When he did, Hans couldn't count. The psychologist realised that the officer was unconsciously giving cues to the horse: he wasn't aware he was doing so, but subtle movements told Hans when to stop. Hans was indeed very clever, but in a different and more sensitive way than portrayed by the officer.

The face is the most important message-giver in the animal kingdom, perhaps because it is the part that meets friends and predators – safe and unsafe – first. Clear signs of acceptance or fear are important for survival. If these messages were confusing, disastrous results might follow.

Very often body language is accompanied by sounds or words. If we receive a mixed message, such as laughter accompanied by clenching the fist, we should believe the body language because it is less likely to be affected by any conscious influence.

As well as sending messages to others, the body is an important source of information for ourselves. We are constantly receiving messages of a physical nature to maintain our status quo. Hunger, thirst, a full bladder, shivering and sweating are all telling us something about the physical needs of the body.

Sometimes the messages radiating from the body are symptoms of an underlying problem. Working too hard may result in headaches, indicating that we should slow down; insomnia may be alerting us to a worried mind. When we become aware of the activity of our body, psychological understanding will result.

Case History

As a boy, Andrew was constantly criticised and made to look foolish by his insecure father. On occasions his father beat him, leaving him scarred physically and mentally. In order to repair the damage, Andrew sought therapy in his twenties and managed to heal much of his childhood legacy.

He came to see me when he was 35 for help with phobias that were causing great problems. We had a number of sessions, but each time he visited his father, he plummeted into a state of anxiety and depression. His father knew what buttons to press to make Andrew feel insecure and worthless.

At one consultation Andrew had a large bruise on the side of his face, but was smiling and looked happier than I'd seen him for a long time.

'What happened to your face?' I asked.

'It's the badge of realisation. I've seen the light.'

Confused, I asked, 'What do you mean?'

'Well, last week I was in the gym boxing and my mind really wasn't there. My guard was down and the other chap kept hitting me. I didn't feel any pain but the word "defence-less" kept going around in my brain. Then he hit me with a right hook to my face and I woke up and boxed really well. After the bout I thought about the word "defenceless" and realised I hadn't kept my guard up in the ring, so I got hurt. I also realised that I'm not keeping my defences up against Dad, so I'm constantly being hurt there too.

'This bruise on my face is a reminder to be aware of the damage Dad can do to me. It is fascinating that my body has taught me dramatically what my mind has known for years. I wish I could keep this bruise for the rest of my life so that when I look in the shaving mirror each morning I could be reminded to keep up my defences for the rest of the day.'

This case is an interesting, if rather extreme, example of how an awareness of the body can help with our behaviour patterns. As body language is both external and internal, awareness enhances our communication in a variety of ways.

Listening to the Body

Body language is a way for emotions to reach the outside world, a way of conveying feelings to others, and a way beyond conscious control to share what is happening within ourselves. It is also a method of learning about ourselves and the needs we have in many different areas of the mind/body complex.

The body stores our memories in a different way from the mind. The mind creates recall through thoughts or images, while the body does so through feelings and bodily expressions. When we recall something frightening, the body feels the fear again, and this feeling creates a series of responses to the systems within the body. Changes in muscular tension, facial expression and blood flow, for example, can be recognised by an observer. The body is speaking without using words.

When we realise that words are only part of the story, we can make a more accurate decoding of the personal messages we send and receive. By learning how the body communicates with us and others, we achieve a much greater understanding and harmony within the mind/body system.

8

Empathy

'Empathy is the power of understanding and
imaginatively entering into another person's feelings.'

COLLINS CONCISE ENGLISH DICTIONARY

To naturally empathetic people the process of entering into
another person's feelings may be one of habit beyond awareness.
But to those who struggle with relationships, cannot understand
their partners, and feel as if they are constantly walking on
eggshells, the process could be a black hole of incomprehension
– like a blind man trying to cross the road, using as his guide
the screech of tyres, the blast of car horns and the screaming of
irate drivers.

Communication at its best is difficult, but when half the
signals given are being misread, it is understandable that problems arise. This chapter explores non-verbal messages, with the
aim of improving communication between those who can and
those who can't empathise.

There are many routes by which messages can be transferred
from one person to another – words, tone of voice, body
language, eye movements, facial expressions . . . All the messages
transmitted are reflecting the thoughts, feelings and attitudes of
the speaker. He may or may not be aware of the diversity of
signals he is sending, but they are all sent nevertheless, and may
be decoded if the receiver is empathetic.

Empathy refers to the transference of emotional messages
between people. Being aware of the emotions of others is

perhaps *the* major factor in communication between individuals.

In any communication there is the factual content transmitted verbally and the emotional content transferred by other means. Communication is said to be congruent when the verbal statement and the body language are the same, and incongruent when these two are conflicting. If we receive a verbal message saying 'Yes' and body language indicating 'No', the latter would be more accurate of the person's true feelings as the body never lies. A client screwing up his face and clenching his fists while saying, 'You know, Brian, I really love my mother,' presents an obvious incongruity. In this case I would take more notice of his body language than his words.

Empathy is a feeling we have about the feelings of others. It may not be rational or logical but it is real. We pick it up from minimal cues radiating from facial expressions, posture, speech components, eye movements or intuition. It is a feeling rather than a logical process – a feeling *for* someone and the state of mind they are experiencing. Its delicacy is such that it can be compared to the mating dance of two butterflies.

For most of my early life my empathy rating was close to zero. I had no idea what *my* feelings were let alone what other people were feeling. I was guided by logic and practicality. Even when I became interested in therapy and was set training exercises in recognising emotions in others, I found it difficult to understand their situation and experiences.

When I started my practice in England my first clients included a woman and her sister, who came to discuss problems with another member of the family. I believed I was very helpful during the consultation and was surprised when the woman rang the following day to cancel her next appointment. When I asked why she was cancelling she said, 'Don't you know, Doctor?'

'No,' I replied in a confused state.

'Didn't you see how angry my sister was with some of the things you said?'

I was in a daze as I hung up the phone. Here I was believing one thing while the opposite was really the case. I thought both women were happy with the consultation, when in fact one – or both – were actually very angry. I sat down to think about this dilemma. If I were to practise in this area of medicine I certainly needed to become aware of the feelings of my patients.

In some strange way my ability to connect to the feelings of others started on that day. I do not know how it happened, but I assume that the ultimatum I gave myself was a key that opened the door to my emotional receptors. It is many years since then and I have seen thousands of patients, so I believe my radar must be working as I haven't had any more incidents like the one with the two sisters.

The Importance of Empathy

Why is empathy so important? How does it help us to know or believe we know how others feel? What happens when this ability is missing? The answer to all these questions lies in one word – understanding. As one patient said to me, 'Being understood is like being loved.'

Understanding the feelings of others is a major part of understanding them as individuals. Peoples' personalities consist of thoughts, feelings and attitudes (the feeling component being the most powerful), so your being accurately connected to their emotions makes them feel as if they are really known by you. If, on the other hand, you acknowledge the facts they are stating but ignore the emotional content, they will feel misunderstood and that you don't know them at all.

What are the components that make up this complex construction labelled empathy? This question seems to produce conflicting answers. Conscious awareness plays a major role, allowing us to notice the emotional messages being sent. On the other hand, the unconscious mechanisms of intuition and gut reaction also play an important part.

Knowing your own feelings is very important too, as it would not be easy to be aware of the emotions of others if you were ignorant of your own. An alexithymic or cool customer (see chapter 3), who is unaware of his feelings, would find it extremely difficult to have empathy with another person. Saddam Hussein, for example, is too egocentric to see empathy as anything but a weakness. At the other end of the emotional spectrum, a highly passionate person might be so involved in their own emotions that they have no time or inclination to notice emotional messages radiated by others. There is also a group more directed to others' needs than their own, called the Jains. This Indian religious sect comprises a very caring group of emotional people who have such sensitivity to every living thing that they wear masks to avoid inhaling and damaging insects, and sweep in front of them as they walk in case they step on an ant.

Empathy is a bi-directional process. If two people, A and B, are communicating empathetically, A will send a subliminal message about his feelings that will be noticed by B. B will then send two messages back – the first being that he has received A's message, and the second being one of his own in response. The process will then be continued with the roles reversed.

This might sound complicated, but it isn't. For empathetic people this process would be happening naturally throughout the day: it is a continuous flow, an exchange occurring beyond conscious awareness. For those who have difficulty relating to others, the process requires conscious effort to read or respond to the signals.

Case History

Janine was happily married, and when a daughter was born she called her Rachel after a favourite aunt on her husband's side. She phoned her parents to break the good news and expected them to visit with love and excitement.

When her mother arrived, Janine knew all wasn't well. Over a cup of tea, her mother angrily said, 'When I heard you'd called her Rachel, I was so upset. Rachel reminds me of concentration camps and gas chambers.'

Janine's mother certainly didn't follow the rules of empathy.

She was not being supportive and understanding to her
daughter in her time of joy. She was not aware of the emotional
response following her words. She was not 'in Janine's shoes'.
She was not reading body language.

Empathy and Gender

Generally, it must be said, women are more in tune with their
feelings than men. They speak more openly about them and are
often more alert to the feelings of others.

Some therapists believe that the ability to empathise is laid
down in childhood. If the mother has problems of her own, has
no time, or is frightened of making mistakes, she is in no position to give her child the attention it requires. Patience, love,
understanding, acceptance, time, confidence, care – all the ingredients of the mother–baby relationship – form the framework
of empathy in the child. Each time the mother looks at her child
in a loving way, the child learns about the security of its own
feelings and the feelings of others.

Studies of a number of adults, ranging from those who had
minimal empathy to those who were very empathetic, showed
that an important factor in their behaviour was the attunement
between them and their mother during childhood. This refers
to the mother's devotion (or lack of it) to her baby and the
nature of the interactions between them.

An attuned mother constantly looks at her baby and reflects
its moods and actions in a positive, reinforcing way. Smiles and
playful behaviour are warmly returned and cuddles given; positive messages are also given to less happy behaviour, such as
scowling, because in this way the baby learns to accept and value
its own feelings and expressions, as well as those of the mother.
This is how empathy is built up over the years and expanded to
others outside the family.

If the mother has difficulty bonding, suffers from post-natal depression or is too busy to give time to the baby, it does *not* learn to appreciate and respect its feelings or the feelings of others. It sends out messages by its body language only to have them ignored or criticised, learning in the process that it is not pleasant or safe to have emotions, and so does not develop self-confidence or empathy.

Adults who exhibit anti-social behaviour have often lacked the learning in childhood that would help them to value their own feelings and those of others. The emotional isolation they suffered leads them to make incorrect assessments about people's reactions and illogical justifications for any anti-social behaviour.

Case History

Edward, a 35-year-old engineer, had difficulties in many areas of his life, but the most troublesome area was relationships. He was brought up by a single working mother and with two older siblings. There was never enough time for him because his mother was either too busy or too tired. He didn't receive the necessary ingredients to allow his emotional skills to develop.

His teenage years were fraught with relationships that never quite succeeded. He took out many girls with whom he thought he was getting on well until they dropped him. He always found fault with the girls to explain the break-up in the relationship.

He married at the age of 25, and problems in the marriage brought him and his wife Terry to my consulting rooms. Terry burst into tears while recounting a litany of complaints about Edward. I noticed he was leaning away from her and looking around the room as tissue after tissue soaked up her tears.

Edward had no idea what was happening in Terry's emotional system. She was giving many signals with her body language, tone of voice and tears, but he did not have the equipment to decode them. His responses related to facts and logic, while she was talking about emotions. They were simply not connecting.

Edward lacked emotional skills because he had learnt none during childhood. He was not to blame – he didn't have a choice of mother. But his mother was not entirely at fault either – she didn't have the choice of spending quality time with her son as he grew. The fact remained, however, that Edward was not able to access internal responses that could help him to understand his wife's pain.

Helping Edward to learn about Terry's emotions, and his own, was a long and difficult process – a little like teaching a severe dyslexic to read. He lived more in his mind than his heart and used logic to deal with life's problems. The saying 'To some men with a hammer everything is a nail' applied perfectly to him. Unfortunately, Terry's emotions were certainly not a nail to be hammered in by Edward's logic.

Achieving Empathy

The famous American psychiatrist Harry Stack Sullivan described empathy as an unverbalised communication process whereby attitudes, feelings and judgements are passed from person to person without ever being publicly articulated. To achieve this state of affairs, the following components are necessary:

Attentive listening. The skill of listening with an open mind, focusing on what is said and really hearing the words and inflections of the speaker (see chapter 20).
Being non-judgemental. This allows the speaker to be free to express any attitude or emotion without fear of criticism.
Standing in the other person's shoes. Imagining how the person feels irrespective of your own views or beliefs. This is the opposite of 'If I were you I would . . .'

Observing. Sensing the minimal cues radiated by body language.
Reflecting. Commenting on messages received for verification.
Mirroring. Reflecting the speaker's body language in your own posture and gestures.
Sensitivity. Having the tact not to be intrusive, respecting personal barriers.
Intuition. Using gut reactions to be aware of the unconscious vibrations radiating from the other person (see chapter 18).
Caring. Being supportive of the other person, focusing on their needs rather than your own.

Empathy allows others to feel justified in their attitude, supported and free to be themselves. It creates a bond of trust and understanding, a respect between partners that unites them on many levels.

9

Factors that Influence Our Emotions

'In order to decide which path to follow,
ask someone who is coming back.'

CHINESE PROVERB

It has been said that our attitudes and actions are based on moving away from pain or towards pleasure. If this is so, and as we *feel* both pain and pleasure, it follows that feelings are integral to our actions and attitudes.

Keeping in mind the pain/pleasure principle, this chapter explores the main factors that influence how we feel, especially those that allow for the possibility of change and improvement. By having feelings that more accurately reflect our situation, we are in a better position to respond according to our abilities and belief systems.

The creation of feelings is a complex matter involving the obvious, the known and the unknown, and forces internal and external. The outlines that follow will help you gain insight into some of these emotions and discover what you are doing (or not doing) that is influencing your own emotions. In this way you will become more aware of the role they are playing in your life.

Feelings from Thoughts

There is a two-way street between thoughts and feelings – they can create one another. In simple terms, the thought process utilises nerve impulses to liberate peptides that result in feelings (see chapter 1).

The theory of state-dependent learning and memory says that our thoughts, learning and memory may be related to the emotional state we are in at the time. For example, if we are enveloped by an intense emotion such as fear, we will have difficulty recalling events from that time unless we return to the frightened state.

This theory is used in therapy when the rational mind states one thing and the emotional mind another. In order to alter the rational thought, we need to go into the original emotional state to allow changes to occur.

Case History

James was on his way to a very important business meeting when he got stuck in a traffic jam on the motorway. He sat in his car, anxious and angry, for 45 minutes. He was late for the meeting, which caused problems at work.

Some time later he found himself becoming very anxious when travelling on a motorway. His emotional mind kept recalling his unpleasant experience even though his rational mind knew it was pointless.

To help James we needed to go back into the emotional state where the idea that motorways cause problems took root in his mind. This state of feelings consisted of anger, frustration, anxiety and guilt, and once he was guided into these emotions, he could re-program his mind to believe that motorways are useful to get from A to B.

This programming would have been much more difficult if he had been in a different state of emotion, such as feeling secure and safe.

Lifting the gloom

Many people are stuck in a rut of emotional gloom: they cannot move forward to pleasure as they are held fast in pain. It is not easy to extract yourself from the quicksand of despair, especially when you have had many experiences that create fear, anger, hopelessness, loss of control and disillusion about yourself or the world. However, there are ways to reach the safety of firm ground, and some of them are discussed below.

Hope is a powerful emotion and can provide the energy to move forward, but do not rely on this alone. Focusing on any positive aspects of the past, present or future provides energy that may lead you in the right direction, and self-praise has also been shown to be beneficial.

One of the best ways to help people out of their rut of doom and gloom is positive support. Sharing thoughts with understanding friends, being listened to by therapists who are not personally involved, doing things in a supportive group – all these can help to improve the internal balance and provide a light at the end of the tunnel.

Forms of Thought

Our thoughts take many forms. By looking at some of them we can gain helpful insights that will help us to tailor our thought processes to our needs or situation.

Representations

Psychologists have a saying: 'The map is not the territory'. This serves to distinguish the reality of what happens (the territory) from our interpretation of what happens (the map).

Sometimes the map is mistaken for the territory, leading us to believe our feelings rather than what we actually observe. (You have only to compare witness statements in a trial to see a good example of this.)

In childhood we need to develop ways of coping with the world and dealing with things we can't comprehend. We make a number of maps to help us avoid pain, pitfalls and punishment and to achieve pleasure, praise and acceptance. We try hard to make maps that work specifically for us, and continue to fine-tune them until they are as effective as possible. Adulthood brings greater ability, power and choices, but some of us continue to use the child's map to deal with the world. Similarly, if you live in London and travel by tube, an Underground map is invaluable. If you then move to Paris and use the same map to navigate the Métro, the results will be disastrous. So it is with life. We need to adjust our maps continually to provide an accurate representation of both our abilities and the situations we experience. The inner world needs to mirror the outer one.

Case History

Shirley felt anxious and guilty whenever she was a few minutes late. The map she carried with her was the sound of her father's voice saying 'Only rude people are late!' She knew as an adult this was not so, as many of her friends were late and they were not rude, but the map was indelibly imprinted in her mind and heart.

When she consulted me we discussed her task, which was to create a new map to fit *her* experiences and beliefs, not those of her father. Over a period of weeks she formulated self-talk to boost her confidence:

'I am a nice, normal woman.'

'I will endeavour to be on time.'

'If I am late, I will accept it as due to circumstances.'

Over time, as she 'brainwashed' herself with the new self-talk, she became much more relaxed about her punctuality.

Shirley learnt that it is necessary to update emotions and beliefs in order to provide the most useful coping mechanism for day-to-day experiences. Julian learnt the same lesson in a different context.

Case History

Julian came to see me for help with failed relationships. He had taken out many girls but after a few months they left him and he couldn't understand why. His friends told him it was his attitude, so he sought my advice.

Julian's father was the headmaster of a boys' school. He was strict and uncompromising, and treated his wife with the same authoritarian approach he used with his pupils. Julian's mother was patient and long-suffering, never complained and accepted her role in life.

At some level this template of relationships was imprinted in Julian's psyche. He had no idea that it could be any other way. He just didn't realise the role that understanding, sharing and caring played in relationships. He was generally surprised when girlfriends left him: in his view, he was behaving normally (just as his father had).

Julian and I spent many months looking at his belief systems ('Men earn the money and women should look after the home', 'A woman shouldn't question a man's reasoning') and checking if they would be suitable for a warm, loving, long-term relationship.

It took a long time and many more failed relationships before Julian was able to see things differently, become aware of his partner's feelings and views, and be able to respect them.

Misinformation

Our emotions are often related to the information we receive, whether it is internal in the form of self-talk, or from external sources. On many occasions we are told things that are factually incorrect, so it is important to separate the right from wrong, and not just take the spoken or written word as fact.

Misinformation causes problems. In the case of our self-talk, unsuitable emotions are created that dominate behaviour. It is important to be aware of what we tell ourselves and to check that the words we use are accurate and helpful.

Metaphor, symbol and analogy

One way we influence our emotions is by using metaphors, symbols and analogies to represent objects and actions. For example, instead of saying someone went into battle, we could say that he roared into battle, implying that he has the qualities of a lion and is very brave.

It is important to ensure the metaphors we use are appropriate and accurate, as they represent our attitudes just as internal maps do. The symbolism becomes imbedded in our psyche and is used as a reference point, displacing the situation itself.

Case History

Ian was concerned about getting married to Fiona. He had lived with her for three years and loved her very much, but he wasn't sure it was right to get married. His parents fought constantly, and whenever he thought of marriage the image that came to mind was of putting his head in a lion's mouth and asking it not to bite him.

We discussed the symbolism of this image, and Ian realised that he was more concerned with the symbol (which had been embedded in his mind since childhood) than marriage itself.

As we looked at the various aspects of his relationship with Fiona, he altered the image to one of 'Building a special house with Fiona'. This allowed him to consider other things that were concerning him. Was it the right time? Could he afford it? Was he ready to settle down?

With this new image, Ian felt he had much more control,

there was no pressure, and he could discuss his views with Fiona in a way that felt comfortable. He was still undecided but believed the new symbol was helpful rather than frightening.

We often translate experiences and attitudes into analogies with familiar activities. For example, a chess player may view his business career as a series of calculated moves; a tennis player may regard relationships as a competitive game; while someone who questions everything may see life as a puzzle.

For people who work long hours, never have time for themselves and have trouble saying 'no', a helpful analogy is a sponge that has absorbed too much water to be useful. In order to increase the capacity of the sponge we need to reduce its content so it can absorb again, and next time round we have to ensure it does not absorb too much.

Comparisons

Feelings are created when we make comparisons, which in some situations can lead to notions of superiority or inadequacy. Comparing our worth to that of others will inevitably lead to feelings of elation or jealousy. The resultant emotion depends on our perspective: is the glass half-empty or half-full?

Another area of comparison is between where you are now and where you would like to be.

When making such comparisons we might focus on specific aspects, ignoring the complete picture, and thus drawing the wrong conclusions. We might also make the mistake of ignoring progress that has occurred in the intervening period.

So many people are too 'hard on themselves'.

Case History

George was an ex-army officer who had retired five years before consulting me. During his army career he had experienced much criticism and punishment from superior officers.

He decided to take up bowls in his retirement, and it was causing him a great deal of stress with resultant indigestion. He worried excessively before each game and constantly blamed himself for mistakes and failures. His family and friends advised him not to take the game so seriously, but their words fell on deaf ears.

George was using comparisons to create his anxiety. He kept recalling decisions and situations that were life-threatening in his army career and applying them to his bowls. He constantly thought he mustn't make a mistake, spoke in terms of failure and consequences, and reprimanded himself if he didn't perform satisfactorily.

His experiences in the army were so powerfully etched in his emotions that they became his major point of reference. It was as if his bowls game were another battle with the same intensity and importance. He was unaware that he was using this comparison, but his attitude and terminology revealed it to be so.

George and I spent many weeks breaking the links between bowls and warfare. We focused on aspects such as friendship, teamwork, exercise, enjoyment, challenge, the game being more important than the result, the fact that others were beginners too and that very little was expected of him.

We changed the aim from 'I mustn't make a mistake and I have to win' to 'I play bowls to meet other people and have fun.'

Over time he learnt to let go of the mantra, 'Success is everything', and replaced it with 'I'm going to have fun'.

In this way his comparisons with army life receded and his stress symptoms disappeared.

Anticipation

We can either look forward to an event or dread it, but in either case the feeling is directly related to our anticipation. Thinking of the future as a glass half-empty will make us feel low: think of it half-full and the reverse will occur. Thoughts of a future event are coloured by the way we feel now.

People who are frightened of flying often say that the time

leading up to the flight is much worse than the flight itself. Fear is created by the anticipation rather than the situation.

Conversely, we can enjoy looking forward to holidays, films or outings, and even if they don't live up to our expectations, we have had the benefit of all the good feelings leading up to them.

Uppers and Downers

Many things influence our emotional well-being, and the text that follows discusses some of the principal reasons for fluctuations in our emotional stability.

The energy bank

Energy is required for the mind/body system to function properly. Just think of expressions such as 'feeling low' or 'on a high' and it's clear that energy plays a major role in how we feel.

It is important to be aware of factors that raise or lower energy levels. A spiral occurs, where anxious attitudes lower our energy, leading to more worries; conversely, positive perspectives create more energy. An increase of energy occurs when we like ourselves, accept ourselves and praise ourselves. We also have a boost of energy when we receive support and encouragement from others. Energy is drained by constant worry, self-criticism, perfectionism, guilt, low self-esteem, feeling isolated or believing we are a failure.

People who are constantly rushing around, under pressure, having no time for themselves may drain their energy to the extent that burnout occurs. Aiming to be always a 'fixer' uses much more energy than being an 'acceptor'. Worrying what other people think, making constant comparisons and being hard on yourself also 'flattens your battery'.

Loving yourself provides positive resources to deal with many things that would otherwise get you down. In fact the bottom line of many people's problems is a lack of self-love. In order to have our emotions in the best possible state, we need to ensure that energy levels are high. To do this we need to be aware of those things that withdraw or deposit energy in our mind/body system.

Chemicals

We all know how our emotions can be affected by chemicals, either those we take or those produced by the mind/body system. Mood-altering substances have become part of our lives in the form of tea, coffee, alcohol, nicotine, food, and drugs legal and illegal.

The chemicals in cigarettes, alcohol and food are used to suppress feelings as well as enhance them. Depressive people often 'self-medicate' with alcohol or drugs to escape the terrible emotions that envelop them. Many more people extol the virtue of a glass of wine or whisky after a hard day at the office to relax and put them in a good mood. Binge-eaters may be unaware that their actions are also based on suppressing intolerable emotions that they can't handle in any other way.

Prescribed drugs play a major role in helping us feel better if we are stressed, phobic, depressed or having panic attacks. Research is discovering more and more chemical receptors related to our emotional states, and developing drugs to alter chemical interactions that affect our mind/body system.

Chemicals that we produce ourselves, such as hormones and endorphins, can profoundly affect the way we feel. Hormonal fluctuations during the menstrual cycle, for example, can produce marked mood swings, as well as a variety of physical symptoms, such as water retention.

Movement

The mind/body system is a complex of thoughts, feelings and intuition, but it is also influenced by movement. A physical workout may be demanding, but the benefits are fantastic.

Dancers and athletes talk of feeling exhilarated and on a high – a result of the endorphins released during exercise.

A swimmer who plods up and down the pool doing his lengths will use different words to describe the benefit he gains – 'I let go of everything, feel calmer, clear my mind, forget my worries.' The repetitive movement of swimming produces a hypnotic effect, but also creates endorphins that alter his mood.

People who jog regularly say how much better they feel after the run. The combination of solitude (or cameraderie when running with a friend), fresh air, competition against the clock, exercise and rhythmic movement all play a role in this mood enhancement.

Going to the gym has now become a favoured pastime for many people. Exercise produces a feeling of well-being because we are doing something for ourselves, something our body needs to keep us looking well and feeling healthy.

Other forms of movement, such as t'ai chi, are not especially energetic, but they still create changes of mood. The slow, specific movements performed in co-ordinated ways create an amazing feeling of well-being. The precision of these movements requires a concentration that produces a paradoxical release.

Starting a form of exercise that suits your needs, personality and time is a great way to boost your emotional well-being because it guarantees an improvement in mood. Try it and see.

Sensory input

When our senses are stimulated our emotions change – we feel different. The extent of this difference depends on the intensity of the stimulation.

The stimulation may be visual – a lovely scene or a painting; auditory – music, poetry or stories; tactile – pleasing textures; olfactory – appealing smells; or tastey – delicious flavours.

In some situations we are bombarded by sensory input, so it is difficult to decipher which sensation is related to our mood changes. For example, during a meal with friends at a restaurant you are receiving sensory stimuli from:

- the tastebuds reacting to the food and drink you are consuming
- the eyes taking in the food and the surroundings
- the ears hearing conversation, music and the noises of other diners
- the nose smelling the food and other aromas
- the emotions in relation to the service, the food you ordered, your fellow diners and the comfort of the seating arrangement

As we are receiving all these stimuli at the same time, it is difficult to decode what may have changed our mood. By learning to recognise what causes us to feel good, we can repeat the feeling whenever we want.

Posture

The way we feel is reflected in the way we look, both facially and physically. The converse is also true – the way we carry ourselves influences the way we feel.

If we feel dejected, we look down, slump our shoulders and let our muscles sag, combining our depressed feeling with depressing posture: they reinforce each other.

If bad posture can make us feel bad, it follows that good posture – head high, shoulders back, chest out, legs straight – will make us feel better.

It could be said that we create an embodiment of our emotions through our posture and attitude. To embody something means to give it tangible form, and the body does this with our emotions. Often our body will respond without our awareness and this is why body language is so important in communication – it is literally telling others how we feel.

Be conscious of what your body is telling you and you have the power to improve your feelings.

Light and climate

It is no exaggeration to talk about 'sunny' personalities: we all feel better when the sun shines. People from hot countries, such as Italy and Africa, are noted for their warmth and outgoing temperament. On the other hand, those from latitudes further north, such as Britain and Finland, tend to be more reserved, perhaps reflecting the cooler and less sunny nature of their climate.

Sunlight is important for physical well-being, not least because its action on the skin produces vitamin D, which is essential for strong bones. However, certain people are so badly affected by lack of sunlight during the dark winter months that they are said to suffer from seasonal affective disorder (SAD). The main symptom of this condition is depression. Fortunately, it can be alleviated by using a light-box to boost exposure to ultraviolet light when most needed.

10

Triggers

'The trigger may be pulled in the present, but
the target remains in the past.'

BRIAN ROET

Numerous factors affect the way we feel, but those most powerful
in releasing the emotions of past experiences are triggers. This
chapter discusses how triggers work and how you can use them
to gain a clearer understanding of your emotions.

Many years ago a number of research papers were written
about emotional states by the US brothers and authors Raymond
and Charles Wolfe. They were particularly interested in the reaction of the stomach lining to stress, but were restricted in their
endeavours because endoscopy, scans and biochemical assays
were not then available. Then they heard about Tom, a slightly
simple youth who had been accidentally shot in the stomach.
The wound had not healed and he was left with a fistula – a
passage from the stomach to the abdominal wall.

Wolfe and Wolfe employed Tom as their laboratory assistant
and set up a research program to study the lining of Tom's
stomach in response to a variety of stressors. They would cause
Tom to be angry, frightened, guilty, sad or disgusted, for example,
and then look into his stomach through the fistula with a small
telescopic instrument. The results showed a definite correlation
between the stressor and gastric secretions: Tom's stomach
became red and produced more acid when he was subjected to
these emotional onslaughts. I am horrified to think of poor Tom

being used as a guinea pig in that way – being frightened and then having either of the brothers peer through a hole into his stomach!

Since then much more research has been undertaken to study bodily responses to certain stimuli. Anything that causes an emotion to occur is called a trigger or inducer. This may be an external occurrence, affecting one of our senses, or an internal occurrence, such as a thought or memory. The trigger acts as a key, gaining access to a specific emotion stored in the mind/body system and bringing it to life so that we feel it again just as we did originally.

This process of emotional release is very important, and well illustrated by the French author Marcel Proust. One day, while having tea with his over-anxious mother, he accepted a madeleine, a small sponge cake, the taste of which triggered a wealth of childhood recollections. This flash of memory changed his life, and he devoted the next 15 years to writing his most famous novel, *A la recherche du temps perdu* (In Search of Lost Time), drawing on memories that surfaced from various triggers – the sound of a teaspoon on a cup, the stiffness of a table napkin, the smell of smoke . . .

All of us can recall times when the triggering process has released intense emotions. Sometimes these are happy and joyous, sometimes negative. We may or may not be aware of the trigger, and we may also be unaware of the situation that caused the emotion in the first place.

Even when we are aware of the circuitry that pushes emotions to the surface, we may find it difficult to prevent them. A repetitive stimulus/response, such as embarrassment when meeting new people, cannot necessarily be controlled, even if we know what originally caused the emotion. The feedback loop (see chapter 6) is difficult to alter, and just the thought of meeting new people may be enough to trigger the system into producing the chemicals and nervous impulses associated with embarrassment. Similarly, circular thoughts or ruminations may act as emotional triggers. The thoughts go round and round in our heads, creating feelings as they go.

Case History

Ashley cannot cope with life. He ruminates constantly about his financial situation following the loss of vast amounts of money on the stock exchange. He is haunted by the thought that if he had sold his shares six years previously, when the idea first occurred to him, he would now be a wealthy man rather than deep in debt.

His mind and emotions are being run by the words 'If only', which trigger self-pity, anger, guilt and depression. He works hard to prevent this vicious cycle, but is constantly reminded of his situation by such things as his friends buying a new car or going on holiday. Ashley realises it is irrational to look back and blame himself, but the 'If only' trigger is too powerful for him, and he is in a constant state of depression and self-recrimination.

In order to break this cycle of anguish, Ashley must learn to block his thoughts and emotions from the 'If only' trigger. He needs to focus his attention on the present and the future, where the trigger has less effect, break the cycle of rumination and put energy into restoring himself to a better financial situation.

Ashley's dilemma has five components that led to his state of depression, and these tend to operate in the emotional system of each and every one of us.

1. **The precipitating factor**. In Ashley's case, this was the loss of his money and the fact that he fell from great wealth to being in debt.

    Such a turnabout has a dramatic effect on thoughts, feelings and lifestyle, and as Ashley waited six years before consulting me, the process of healing and integration had been arrested and replaced by circular ruminations.

    Precipitating factors can be major or trivial, but the result is life-changing.

'Why are you divorcing your wife?'

'Because she never puts the top on the toothpaste.'

The precipitating factor is blamed, analysed and clung to like a dog with a bone, but it is often only a minor part of the story.

2. **The emotional pool.** In 1865 a French biologist called Claude Bernard described the inside of our mind/body complex as the *milieu interieur* (interior environment). This encompasses the factors: chemical, physical and nervous, that create thoughts and emotions and control all the different systems in the body. I call the emotional components of the *milieu interieur* the 'emotional pool' – the place where we store the emotions felt during our lifetime. This pool will be sweetly flavoured by happy experiences and soured by those that cause distress.

As all the systems of the mind/body complex are involved in feedback loops to maintain the status quo (see chapter 6), the emotional pool is an integral part of our response to circumstances that we encounter.

In Ashley's case, I learnt he had a very successful father, who was head of a large firm of accountants. His brother was a successful lawyer with a smart house and expensive cars. The message Ashley received in childhood was that success and respect were judged by the amount of money earned. He received praise and love when he did well financially, and rejection when he didn't. In his own words, 'Money meant success, respect, and proof that I was as good as my father.' So Ashley's emotional pool was heavily biased towards equating self-worth in terms of cash. When he was doing well, amassing his fortune, he felt fantastic, considered himself as good as anyone else and believed others saw him as an equal. When he lost his money his opinion of himself plummeted and he believed others felt the same.

3. **Character and attitude.** These are moulded by upbringing, the values of others, self-belief systems and ideas. In Ashley's case, these were focused more on external achieve-

ments than internal understanding. His energy over the years had been expended on making money. He was a workaholic who had no quiet times of contemplation, so he was emotionally out of balance.

4. **Feedback loops.** As described in Chapter 6, feedback loops are circular processes that reinforce a particular thought pattern or behaviour.

In Ashley's case the 'If only' trigger had him in an endless circle of recrimination and negative emotions that was going nowhere. This was reinforced by his childhood experiences and a belief system that told him money was everything.

By becoming aware of the system maintaining our problems, we can instigate change to make improvements and direct us to more successful outcomes.

5. **Unconscious mechanisms.** We sometimes find ourselves in low moods for no apparent reason. We do not know of any trigger that may have caused the mood and are mystified how it has happened to us. In fact, a change is occurring in the *milieu interieur*, caused by something beyond our conscious awareness. It may be something we have seen but not noticed, a thought that was triggered but not attended to, leaving the resultant emotion.

By being aware of these five components, you can have a greater insight into the way emotions take control, determine if they are negative or inappropriate, and learn to wrest control from them.

Case History

Mavis, a 36-year-old housewife, sought help for a sudden change in mood that made her aggressive towards her husband. It was completely out of character, and although she and her husband had talked at length about the problem, no obvious cause was discovered.

We talked about her past history, and the main item of

note was that she had been molested by a schoolteacher when she was ten. He had threatened violence if she told anyone, so she had kept it a secret until she was married, aged 23, when she discussed it at length with her husband and felt that the situation had been resolved.

We discussed any experiences that might have caused her mood change and she stated that nothing unusual had happened in the last month. I asked her if there were any future events that might be relevant, and after thinking for a while, she replied, 'No. The only thing happening is that my daughter Cecily is having her birthday next week.'

'How old will she be?'

'Ten.'

Her body language changed as she said this and she fell silent. Then she asked, 'Do you think it is possible that Cecily's tenth birthday has triggered memories about when I was ten and that terrible thing happened?'

'It is certainly possible. Your memory may well have stored that experience in such a way that those intense emotions were released in a protective way towards Cecily. Maybe your anger towards the teacher from all those years ago is being re-directed towards your husband. If this is so, it would be worth thinking about realising that Cecily is separate from you and that her situation is in no way related to your experience.'

Over the next two visits Mavis had further insight via thoughts, feelings and dreams about the connection between her traumatic experience 26 years previously and her present mood swing associated with her daughter's tenth birthday. These insights also helped in other ways when aggression occurred in her life. She was able to trace her anger back to her childhood experience, and this gave her a control that had previously been absent.

While triggers most commonly produce emotional responses, they can also provoke physical reactions. An interesting example of this was described to me by my friend Caroline.

Case History

Thirty years previously Caroline had given birth by Caesarean section to her daughter Suzie. A week before our meeting, Suzie herself had given birth to a little boy, but there had been difficulties with the labour. During this time Caroline naturally felt very anxious, but was astonished to find that her old Caesarean scar became inflamed and weepy.

Was this just a coincidence, or was the inflammation triggered by an emotional response to her daughter's labour?

All the senses can act as triggers to our emotions, and everyone, I believe, is susceptible to some stimulus or another. Perhaps certain music recalls a happy occasion, or a photo reminds you of a disastrous holiday. Maybe the smell of a perfume evokes a particular relationship. Triggers are very specific and tend to relate to just one aspect of an experience. That perfume for example, could have many happy associations, but it might trigger only a sad feeling from the end of the relationship. Whatever the situation, the trigger flies us back through time until it targets the past experience that connects with the present-day one.

Understanding the trigger mechanism can provide valuable insights to understanding emotions.

11

Memory – the Fount of All Knowledge

'A man's memory is bound to be a distortion of his past in accordance with his present interests, and the most faithful autobiography is likely to mirror less what a man was than what he has become.'

FAWN BRODIE, AMERICAN WRITER

The memory is an amazing function of the mind, involved in the storage and retrieval of experiences. It starts at birth, perhaps even in the womb or a previous life, and continues until we die. It is a major component in our survival, helping us to recognise friend from foe and good from bad. It also plays an important role in our attitudes, beliefs and behaviour, so it is useful to understand the variety of mechanisms involved in remembering.

How We Remember

The process of remembering involves several stages that are often interwoven with our emotions.

1. An external experience is recorded by one or more of the senses.
2. This stimulus is then encoded – packaged in a specific manner – for storage.
3. The encoded message is stored in a variety of ways in the

unconscious mind – as a fact, an emotion, a survival mechanism or a repressed memory.

4. At a later date it is released into consciousness by a trigger. This process is called retrieval.

Factual memories

A simple, routine experience containing minimal emotion, such as the daily journey to work, could be recorded factually, which means that the detail is forgotten: one journey blurs into another. The mind cannot retain all the information it receives, so it discards situations not worthy of recall.

Emotional memories

Experiences stored emotionally fall into two categories. The first contains resolved emotions, which are feelings that gradually diminish in intensity; the emotional content is reduced while the factual content remains. This process is called resolution. Recalling a resolved emotion brings less and less feeling, so tears may be replaced by sadness for example. In this way we are no longer emotionally stuck at the time of the original experience, but can move on or come to terms with what has happened. We are able to recall *how* we felt but are not overwhelmed by the emotion.

The grieving process illustrates how emotions can be resolved. It begins with anguish, and progresses through disbelief, questioning, anger and guilt to acceptance. Resolution allows us to reduce the intensity of emotions stored in the emotional pool and to progress through life without the burden of painful, out-of-date emotions.

The second category contains unresolved emotions, which are feelings that have not been successfully processed. When experiences are too traumatic to be dealt with they remain in their original state, frozen in time. In this situation I often use hypnosis to explore the client's unconscious mind and determine if the emotion is out of date, being based on earlier experiences.

Accessing the emotion brings it to the surface and allows the process of resolution to be set in motion.

Case History

Albert was in tears as he discussed the death of his eight-year-old daughter Helen. She had died 30 years previously after being hit by a car while crossing the road to greet him. She was on a life-support system for three days, and he relived his distress as he talked about the phone call that requested permission to turn it off.

The anguish stored in Albert's body had remained undiminished for 30 years.

'I just can't get over it. The thought of that day and the loneliness that followed starts intense grief and I can't control it,' he said.

Albert had stored the tragic loss of Helen in a special compartment in his mind and heart, and time had been unable to gain access and dilute the pain. Now, however, he wanted to let it go and move on, so his doctor prescribed anti-depressant tablets and referred him to me for therapy. (This combination often works very well.)

He was very open and honest about his attitude, beliefs and emotions. He wanted to let go of the pain and remember Helen as the bright little girl who gave him so much pleasure before the accident. My aim was to help him focus on other aspects of Helen's life, moving the spotlight in his mind away from the accident and life-support system, and on to the happy experiences before that time. In short, I aimed to help him reduce the painful emotional component in his memory and retain the facts and emotional experiences of earlier times.

Albert was very motivated and able to visualise well: his imagination allowed him to conjure up images and feelings of past experiences. He benefited by being able to express his feelings and thoughts, and was surprised that the tears

decreased with each session. He discussed the wide variety of
feelings that had remained in storage – anger, bewilderment,
guilt, fear – and released them so that he could focus on more
positive aspects of Helen's life, as well as the life he and his
wife were leading in the present. He remarked that he had
never allowed himself to be really happy because of the guilt
and sadness he felt at Helen's death.

The combination of anti-depressants and therapy proved
very effective. After seven sessions Albert declared he could
cope with life in a much less tortured way and no longer
needed to see me. His GP decided to maintain the anti-
depressants for a further six months, and Albert agreed to
contact me if he needed to.

This sad case illustrates how traumatic memories can
remain unaltered for many years, dominating our life, halting
progress, preventing us living in the present and reducing our
enjoyment. By bringing them to the surface and sharing,
facing and expressing them, resolution can occur.

Unresolved emotions are similar to live electrical wires – vulnerable to short circuit when triggered by similar experiences.
Resolution creates an insulation, protecting the wires from
causing further shocks.

How do we know if a traumatic experience is resolved or not?
In simple terms, if recall is accompanied by an intense emotion,
this indicates that resolution of the initial feeling has not
occurred. When I asked Albert about his daughter (see page 112)
he immediately burst into tears, showing that the emotional
component of his memory was still intense. Whenever I ask a
client about a past experience and tears roll down their cheeks,
I know that unresolved emotions are still stored in their unconscious. If they comment about the incident in a factual manner,
it is evident that resolution has occurred.

What Determines Resolution?

- The intensity of the original experience.
- The emotional age and state of mind at the time.
- Powers, strengths and controls available to deal with the experience at the time.
- The character of the person.
- Related experiences that had occurred previously.
- Supportive relationships that allowed expression and discussion of the emotions involved.
- The decision to avoid or confront the experience.
- The length of time the experience continues and, whether it is repeated or not.
- Whether therapy or counselling is sought.

Survival mechanisms

A unique category in the storage/retrieval system occurs when we encounter circumstances believed to be life-threatening. It is as if evolution has designed this process for survival, separating it from the way we deal with everyday events.

These special memories are kept in the emotional equivalent of an aeroplane's black box, protected from interference by our logical conscious minds. They differ markedly from memories that are resolved and diluted with time.

Any perceived threat to life needs to be dealt with urgently and recorded in such a way that future recognition and action occur instantaneously. This protective mechanism acts in a reflex way in order to avoid any delay from conscious analysis and decision-making. The associated emotion is fear, as this produces an active and alert state capable of dealing with situations threatening our survival.

The black box seals the incident in such a way that there is no contact from the rest of the mind; it is unavailable for analysis and judgement, and is stored in its original form and intensity. The fact that time is passing, situations changing and our powers increasing does not filter through its airtight walls.

Difficulties arise from this storage/retrieval system when the original incident becomes out of date, no longer life-threatening and inapplicable to our situation. As it is unresolved, it is latently sensitive to triggers and continues to remind us emotionally of the obsolete experience. We are needlessly shocked into terror and activity when present-day triggers reactivate old memories.

Case History

Tim, a 50-year-old father of two, consulted me for help with panic attacks that occurred whenever he attempted to go swimming. He had tried to use will-power, but with no success, he was taking tablets from his doctor, but they weren't helping; and he had read books on phobias and listened to relaxation tapes, all to no avail.

Tim and I decided to look for the cause of his fear and discovered that he had been ducked under water by his friends on a beach holiday when he was eight years old. He had no conscious recollection of this until we used the affect bridge (see chapter 24) to follow his frightened feelings back in time.

At the time of his ducking he thought he would die. Even though it lasted only a few seconds, it seemed much longer, and this memory was stored in the black box in order to help survival and prevent a recurrence of that terrible ordeal. Every time Tim went near the sea or a swimming pool he triggered the defence mechanism of panic attacks to prevent him drowning. The unconscious was still acting as if he was eight years old because time had not infiltrated the black box.

Therapy was aimed at informing his unconscious that he was old enough to look after himself – he did not need protecting as the eight-year-old did. He took swimming lessons, being very cautious and progressing from the wading pool only when he felt comfortable. It took a number of months for Tim to be able to go into the shallows at the seaside, but by then the power of past memories had been lost and he was in control of his life once more.

Repressed memories

As the mind cannot remember everything, it filters out those things that are less relevant to our lives. Every day we consign thousands of experiences to the 'forgettory' so that we can retain the essential ones. In time, even these essential memories may drift beyond recall, allowing the mind the freedom and space to deal with present-day events. This evolution from remembering to forgetting occurs naturally with the passage of time.

Repression of memories is a completely different process: it is an active one, where the experience is consigned to the unconscious as a protective device. The most common reason why this process is invoked is the belief that the memory will be overwhelming, causing us to lose control.

Repressed memories are stored in the unconscious in a latent form accessible to triggers that may reawaken them. This reawakening will affect emotions, attitudes, beliefs and behaviour, even though we may have no conscious awareness of the repressed memories' content or even their existence. The adult Tim was affected by his childhood experience in the form of panic attacks when he approached water, but he had no rational explanation for them. The rationality was stored in his unconscious in the form 'Tim nearly died by drowning, so we will protect his life by giving him panic attacks'. Repressed memories are stored in the unconscious as a protective mechanism, but on many occasions they cause intrusive and upsetting emotions without creating any real benefit.

State-dependent Learning

What we remember and how we remember it may well depend on the state of mind we are in at the time of the experience. It is known that in times of acute fear or desperation we go into a trance-like state to deal with the trauma. If problems follow these situations, it is often necessary to go back into a trance-like state to 'unlearn' the learning that occurred.

The concept of state-dependent learning (see chapter 9), means that if we learn something in one state of mind it is easier to gain access to the memory if we return to that state. Many therapies make use of this fact to enable clients to develop altered states of mind to rid themselves of traumatic memories.

Moods, too, play a major role in our recalling ability. Volunteers in an experiment were shown either happy or sad films, and then shown a film containing both happy and sad experiences. Upon questioning, those in a happy mood recalled more happy experiences than the others and vice versa. Mood is important in two stages of the storage/retrieval system: first at the time of encoding, and then at the time of recall. This is called mood-contingent recall and goes some way to explaining why there is such a diversity of recollections from people viewing the same incident. It may be that an emotional marker is attached to the memory as it is stored, so recall of that memory is easier if our emotional state is similar to the marker.

Post-traumatic Stress Disorder (PTSD)

This condition represents a unique set of responses relating to intense trauma. When encoding occurs normally it is associated with a 'time tag' similar to the emotional marker discussed above, enabling us to recognise when the incident occurred. In PTSD the initial trauma is so intense that the body produces cortisol to deal with the shock. This has the side-effect of preventing the time tag being attached to the memory. As a result, sufferers have flashbacks where the trauma is so vividly recalled that it seems to be happening in the present: the time of the event has been lost by the effect of the cortisol. These flashbacks cause intense distress because the situation is relived again and again with no loss of intensity.

Subliminal Messages

Messages that enter our memory subconsciously are described as 'subliminal', from the Latin words *sub*, meaning 'under', and *limen*, meaning 'threshold'. They penetrate beneath our threshold of consciousness, and being inaccessible to rational thought, are processed and stored by our unconscious. Recall can occur but it tends to be in the form of a feeling rather than a conscious thought.

Like other memories, subliminal messages are recalled as positive or negative, depending on the state of mind in which they were received. The feelings they arouse may be experienced as gut reactions with no logical association, but this does not diminish their importance in influencing our attitudes and decisions. Lack of logic does not mean they are of little value.

Learning from Experience

Experiential learning is the basis for growth in both humans and animals. From birth to death we aim to make use of what happens to us so that we can move towards pleasure or away from pain. This learning can occur on a factual or emotional basis.

If we do something and it results in a failure, we aim not to repeat the experience, and devise other methods to achieve more successful outcomes. This seems very obvious, but unfortunately some people are unable to put it into practice: they keep repeating the same mistakes again and again.

The reason for this behaviour is that they are unable to gain access to past experiences because their emotional memory is blocking the pathway to their rational memory.

Case History

Matthew consulted me to help with presentations at work. Every week he had to give a five-minute presentation to ten people. Every week he was successful, but he was always terrified he would dry up and be unable to speak.

The reality of the situation is as follows:

- Matthew is competent to give presentations.
- Experience shows that he is able to do this task.
- His memory fails to remind him that he can.
- The overriding emotion of fear dictates his attitude.
- He is not learning from experience.

The process occurring in Matthew's mind/body system is:

- Somewhere in the past he had a frightening experience while speaking to a group.
- The fear has been stored in his memory to such an extent that it blocks any future positive events that may be similar.
- Every time he has to give a presentation it is like the first time. Successful presentations are not recorded in his mind and are unavailable for recall on an emotional level. He hasn't forgotten them, and when asked can remember them, but they do not interact with his feelings and so do not diminish his fear. He is not learning from experience.

The work Matthew and I did was connecting his successful presentations (of which there were many) to an appropriate emotion. In this way we began to link experiences to appropriate feelings and have them stored in his memory as such.

His homework was to go over each and every presentation and have a suitable feeling. He then spent time making sure this connection was maintained, and tested the linkage the next day by recalling that specific presentation and noting if the appropriate feeling was still connected to it.

In this way Matthew 'rewrote' his experience/memory

storage and reduced the fear that was being attached, replacing it with an appropriate feeling. He was actually beginning to learn from his experiences.

In conclusion, it is important to remember that emotional memories play a major role in our attitudes and behaviour. The state of mind at the time of encoding, our character, confidence and power, and the ability to be in control all play a role in how traumatic events may alter our future. By learning more about these processes we can make improvements and let go of the baggage of unresolved traumatic memories, helping our journey through life to be easier.

PART II

Problems with Emotions

12

Overwhelming Emotions

'It's like being swamped by a tidal wave – I become enveloped, submerged, suffocated and lose control completely when the panic takes over.'

PATIENT'S DESCRIPTION OF A PANIC ATTACK

Having learnt what emotions are in Part I, it's now time to look at the problems they can create, particularly when they get out of control.

Attitude and behaviour are influenced by the way thoughts work in conjunction with emotions. When in harmony they enable us to achieve our full potential, but if either dominates, the balance and communication are lost and we fail to achieve our aims.

When emotions take over, our logical perspective is blocked – we 'lose our senses' or 'go out of our mind'. This is described by Daniel Goldman in his book *Emotional Intelligence* as 'emotional hijacking', a state where feelings dominate and exclude rationality. Phrases such as 'paralysed by fear', 'drowned in sorrow' and 'racked by guilt' suggest some of the situations in which the hijacking occurs.

These strong emotions share a powerful vocabulary with natural disasters, such as floods, hurricanes and bush fires, which swamp, engulf or rage with disastrous consequences when out of control. In fact, emotional flooding is a natural phenomenon in childhood, demonstrated in tantrums, sulking and sibling rivalry. Learning emotional balance and control is an essential part of growing up.

When our thoughts are swamped by emotions, the
balance is lost.

However, not all emotional overload is negative: we seek and enjoy it in situations such as horror movies, frightening fairground rides, football matches and passionate love affairs. These emotional hijackings provide excitement, limiting their effects to the activity concerned. Those that cause problems are of a different character and take over against our will.

Emotional flooding that leads clients to seek therapy causes restrictions, fear and concern, creating problems in many different aspects of life, from the workplace to the home. Emotions involved in these areas tend to be fear, anxiety, shyness, rage, guilt, jealousy and shame, and when let loose without the restraining influence of logic 'all hell breaks loose'.

Thoughts and feelings are used to deal with any experience, but as they are separate powers with different perspectives, different histories and a different bias, their reactions may not be congruent, so internal negotiation takes place. 'I think I'll do this but I feel like doing that' provokes a debate that ideally utilises information from both sources to achieve the most suitable and up-to-date response. When our thoughts are swamped by emotions, this balance is lost, causing attitude and behaviour to suffer.

Case History

Emma clearly demonstrated that emotions drowned her logic. This 14-year-old girl came to see me with a fear of birds, especially pigeons. She had been frightened of birds for as long as she could remember, and five years ago the situation became worse following an experience in Trafalgar Square when pigeons surrounded her and she ran in panic to escape them.

Since that time she had always been on her guard against birds, and stayed in her room for much of the holidays if there were any birds in the area. Her parents could see the situation becoming worse, so they sought my help. Over a number of sessions we learnt what was happening inside Emma's mind/body complex that resulted in her terror:

- When she felt safe and there were no birds in sight, or only one in the distance, she had a 'tape' in her head saying, 'Birds are not a problem. They are not interested in me and will fly away if I clap my hands.' This tape created a calm feeling in her stomach.
- When a bird came close or 'looked' at her she felt panicky in her stomach and wanted to run away. The calming words in her head were 'drowned by the fear', so she could not hear them. The panicky feeling built up to a level of terror and she had to run away because the feeling was so intensely unpleasant. As she ran, the feeling became less, but she was left trembling and shaken, even more determined to avoid birds in future.

Advice and comments from friends and family had reinforced the logical calming tape in her head, but this was lost when panic swept through her body. We used hypnosis to analyse this process and discovered that the feeling of terror travelled from her feet to her head via an imaginary tube. The technique we used to neutralise this process involved having the logical message travel down the tube from her head and calm the fear in her feet.

We put this theory into practice by searching the surrounding parks for pigeons (you can never find one when you want one) to enable Emma to be in full control as she edged nearer and nearer to the birds. A number of anxious moments, panics and fleeings occurred, but gradually she was able to reverse the emotional flooding and allow logic to prevail.

Some months later I received a photo of Emma feeding a pigeon. She had a distinct look of satisfaction on her face.

We can be aware when emotional hijacking is in progress by noticing thoughts and statements that are more like illogical excuses than rational reasons. Joy, for example, went to ridiculous lengths to defend her emotional stance when we discussed her fear of sharks.

'Do you ever go swimming in the sea, Joy?'

'No. I'm never sure if there is a shark lurking there.'

'But there are no sharks around the English coast: no one has ever been attacked there.'

'That doesn't matter. What if a shark swam from another country? You couldn't guarantee that wouldn't happen.'

'How about swimming in a pool?'

'No, I wouldn't do that in case a shark had been put in the pool by mistake.'

'But it wouldn't survive in chlorinated water.'

'It may be a genetically modified shark.'

As this conversation with Joy proved, offering logical answers to emotional logic rarely has any beneficial effect.

Emotional Flooding

When emotional flooding occurs we undergo changes in personality, body language and internal dialogue. Recollections of the situation contain comments such as 'I just lost it' and 'I don't know what came over me'.

This happens when the overloading occurs acutely, from a specific trigger. When it is chronic or long term, we adapt and it becomes incorporated into our personality, making us unaware of its influence.

In the acute situation it is quite true to say that we 'go out of our mind' because we succumb to our feelings. These intense changes are accompanied by self-talk that reinforces the feeling and adds fuel to the fire. This attitude is illustrated by the joke about a man who wishes to borrow a ladder from a neighbour a few doors away. He has a feeling that the man is miserable and may not lend the ladder. As he walks down the road he says to himself, 'He's a mean old so and so. He refused to lend a spade to Bill a few weeks ago, so I bet he'll make some excuse. I'll feel silly and humiliated. It's a complete waste of time asking.'

On arriving at the house he rings the bell and as the man opens the door shouts at him, 'You can keep your stupid ladder – I don't want it anyway!'

Ruminations

The thoughts and self-talk that go round and round in our mind reinforcing a belief system are called ruminations because, like ruminant animals that regurgitate and re-chew food, we mull over thoughts time and again. During this process they become interlinked with powerful feelings, one reinforcing the other.

Case History

Tanya suffered from intense jealousy. Her fiancé Louis was fed up with her doubts and fears, so they came to see me for help with their relationship. Tanya admitted it was illogical and unreasonable but complained with tears in her eyes that she just couldn't help it. The sequence of events occurring in Tanya's mind were as follows:

- Basic self-doubt that she is not good enough for Louis and he will discover this and leave her. Previous broken relationships have lessened her confidence and self-worth.
- Louis is very popular and confident. He has had many long-term relationships and has always been the person to finish them. He continues to express his love for Tanya but she doubts he is being honest.
- A trigger occurs, such as Louis being ten minutes late or forgetting to ring Tanya.
- The trigger causes a wave of jealousy to sweep through her body, an intense mixture of fear and anger. The feeling takes over and she loses contact with logical thoughts and explanations.
- She begins to ruminate negative thoughts: 'I always knew it would happen. I'm sure he's found someone else. He never really loved me. I'm not good enough for him.' These thoughts reinforce the feelings of fear and anger.
- She sees pictures in her mind of Louis happy with another woman. Memories of boyfriends who have left her flood into her mind/body complex. When reality intrudes and Louis returns smiling, those internal influences go away – until the next time.

In order to halt this cycle of anguish there are a number of interventions that can be made. They are not easy because the power of emotional overload means that we lose many of the strengths that give us a balanced perspective. It requires time and effort to change the mechanisms producing and maintaining the flooding but it can be done. The techniques are similar to a survival pattern when flood waters swirl around us, the aim is to prevent being dragged down.

1. Learn to be aware. Awareness is of prime importance if we are to make a change or take control. It allows us to be pro-active rather than reacting to feelings and ruminations. Awareness helps us find safe ground in the flood. Prevention is often better than cure.
2. Challenge the negative ruminations with facts, experiences and balanced arguments. Be aware of negative or anxiety-producing words and phrases such as should, must and ought to, 'everyone knows', 'he will never', 'it always happens to me'.
3. Slow down. Emotional take-over often speeds the thinking process and creates a racing mind that can precipitate a disaster. By slowing your thoughts and actions you are allowing yourself to calm down, giving yourself space for rational thoughts to intervene.
4. Create a distraction (see chapter 23) or an involvement so that ruminations can't take hold. Go to the gym, take up a hobby, exercise, garden, anything that will take your mind off it even for a little while.
5. Postpone conclusions until you have gathered more information. There are always two sides to a story.
6. Use reframing (see chapter 23) to see the situation from a more positive perspective.
7. Accept the situation for the time being – 'I'm feeling jealous and that is all right for now. Later on this will pass over and I'll restore myself to a calmer state.'
8. Look back over similar situations and outcomes. What can you learn from these experiences that may be relevant to the present one?
9. Note components of the emotional pool that may be triggered to cause flooding. Check whether these are suitable to influence your reactions. Focus on other emotions and attitudes that may be more appropriate or helpful.

10. Seek help from counsellors or therapists, and if necessary, ask your doctor for temporary medication to help you over a difficult patch.

By following these points, it is possible to restore the heart/head balance and gain control again.

13

Feelings that Block Intentions

'Many people are stubborn in pursuit of the pathway,
few in pursuit of the goal.'

PROVERB

Just as feelings that are out of control can cause problems, so can feelings that block what we wish to do. This chapter explores some of those emotions that place restrictions on us and looks at ways of overcoming them.

The word 'emotion' implies action, yet there is no doubt that some emotions prevent actions rather than encourage them. How often do we say to ourselves, 'I would love to do that but I feel too scared/guilty/jealous/shy to do it'? Our desires and feelings are often pulling us in different directions.

Case History

John was 15 when his worried mother brought him to me for help. She was very concerned about his health, even though he was not suffering from any illness. John's problem was that he wouldn't eat anything but pizza: he felt disgust if anything other than pizza was served to him.

For some unknown reason, from the age of ten John had resisted his family's enticements to eat a variety of food: he would allow nothing but pizza to pass his lips. No matter how often they nagged or asked why, John remained resolute in his attitude. Bribery, coercion, ridicule, punishment, scorn . . . all failed to move him. Family life was disrupted by arguments, mealtime battles, threats and tears, but his mouth refused to open for anything but pizza.

John was very reluctant to talk about his problem with me. He felt well and saw no reason why he should change his diet and explore the culinary world. He liked pizzas and couldn't see why everybody was getting upset about his eating habit. He was nervous about any other food in case he didn't like it; meat, fish and vegetables caused him to feel fear and disgust, and he knew he would be sick even if he tried the smallest morsel. He wanted peace, an easy life, but was constantly surrounded by anger and turmoil, especially from his mother at mealtimes.

Discussion with John was limited: he was defensive and reticent and saw me as an instrument of his mother, attempting to make him do something he didn't want to. *He* didn't have a problem, his family did; if everyone would leave him alone, all would be well.

John didn't attend his second consultation, and when I spoke to his mother she told me he had refused to visit me again, locking himself in his room when the appointment approached. He wanted to be left alone to get on with his life without all the nagging that had upset him for years.

John's situation is an example of how emotions can block our natural behaviour and cause difficulties by removing choices. He apparently had choices when it came to food – he could choose anything – but in reality his feelings of fear and disgust blocked his access to choice.

I have no idea how John's fears developed. They may have been caused by a particular experience, underlying timidity or something that was said, any of which could have grown over the years to block a pathway to his rational thinking. My observation was that his motivation was non-existent and his health seemed fine. My hope was that in time he would venture out from behind his wall of fear and disgust, perhaps aided by peer pressure, and explore the culinary world. My thoughts were that in time he would try different foods, find them palatable and add them to his basic diet of pizza so that choice would become a reality rather than illusion. My belief was that the real problem existed between John and his mother: the battleground they chose to fight on was pizza, but the 'real problem' was something else.

It has been observed that the person with the problem is the one who is complaining. If this is so, then John's mother had the problem. I did ask if she would like to come and talk to me about 'John's problem' but she declined.

Looking Beyond the Problem

The book *Who Moved My Cheese?* is a story about mice in a maze who get cheese from the same spot every day. One day the cheese is not there and each mouse reacts differently to this event. Some search throughout the maze for new cheese; others wait for a while in the hope that the cheese will return, and when it doesn't they go looking for it; the remainder are too nervous to explore and wait in vain for the cheese to come back.

One of the questions posed in this story is: 'What would you do if you were not frightened?' This is interesting because it focuses on an outcome rather than on what is preventing the outcome. Too often but attention is directed towards the problem or what is causing it, and we become entangled in the problem rather than in finding a solution.

Like the timid mice in the story, we may be entangled in a particular aspect of a problem, such as fear, and be unable to look beyond it.

'Why am I frightened?'
'What caused my fear?'

'How will I get over my fear?'

'What will they think of me if I don't lose my fear?'

'Isn't it terrible I'm so scared?'

All these questions are directed at one aspect of the problem – fear. 'What would I do if I was not frightened?' ignores the fear and makes us look beyond it. It directs our energy towards finding a solution. This creates a fear-free state of mind that allows us to address the problem with purpose, confidence and hope.

If you have a problem, look at the emotion it creates and that gets in the way of your wishes. Ask yourself, 'What would I do if I were not guilty/jealous/worried/shy/enraged/anxious?' It's a liberating approach.

Case History

Sarah was jealous – so jealous that the feeling consumed much of her life and prevented her enjoying time with Paul, her husband of four years.

The cause of Sarah's jealousy occurred ten years before she consulted me. She was engaged to be married to Richard but one month before the wedding a knock on the door revealed a very pregnant woman claiming that Richard was the father of her child. Pandemonium ensued, the wedding was called off and Sarah became deeply depressed. As time passed, she formed the belief that no man could be trusted, and the seeds of jealousy were sown.

Five years later she fell in love with Paul, but was terrified of starting another relationship that she 'knew' would end in anguish. She was torn between her love for Paul and the internal tape that kept repeating 'no man can be trusted'. Eventually she decided to marry Paul and their relationship was fine in every respect except her jealousy. Every moment they were apart her mind filled with ruminations:

'Why did my fiancé cheat on me?'

'How can I be certain Paul isn't seeing someone else?'

'Men are different from women and driven by sex.'

'The marriage is too good: something must go wrong.'

'I am not good enough for Paul – he will leave me for someone else.'

These thoughts were accompanied by anger towards Richard and fear about Paul. She used any experience, item of information or gossip to fuel her jealousy.

During our discussions we focused on Sarah's erroneous beliefs, her lack of confidence, the fact that Paul was not Richard, generalisations she made about men and positive evidence that all was well in her relationship. We challenged her expectations and brought reality into her perspective. We talked about the difference between possibilities and probabilities, helping her to realise she had confused the two, and focusing on the probability that Paul was behaving in a trustworthy manner, exactly as he said he was. We talked about being an acceptor for the time being so that she could enjoy all the different aspects of their relationship and realise that jealousy was fixing nothing. She spent time between sessions imagining what life would be like if she weren't jealous. Initially, she found this difficult, but in time came to realise from evidence that Paul was 'different from other men'.

Paul also came to some sessions and discussed his feelings about Sarah's jealousy. Over a number of months the intense fire consuming Sarah became a small flame, irritating but tolerable. She became less emotional and more rational, allowing the experience of ten years previously to drift into the past and not influence her present situation.

Some useful points can be learnt by comparing the pizza-eating John and jealous Sarah. To the casual observer both had problems requiring attention to make their lives easier, but their attitudes and outcomes were vastly different.

John
- denied he had a problem
- lacked motivation
- accepted the status quo
- provided no energy for change
- may well have been diverting the real problem onto the pizza conflict
- remained as he was

Sarah
- took responsibility for her problem
- realised it was interfering with her life
- was prepared to discuss the problem and seek help
- was motivated to change
- put in time and effort to improve
- achieved success

Many emotions prevent us achieving our potential by limiting choices and diverting us from our goals, just as in the story of Ulysses the sirens diverted sailors off their course and onto the rocks of destruction. It is not easy to deny the powerful calls of fear, shyness or jealousy as they steer us away from rational thinking, but it is possible to overcome these emotional blocks. By being aware of their presence, learning how they came to be part of you, improving the connection between logic and emotion, sharing your feelings with others and utilising support you can relegate the feeling to the past and change direction towards a more rational approach.

14

Emotional Blackmail

A Jewish mother gave her son two ties for his birthday.
The following week he visited her wearing one of the ties.
As she opened the door to greet him, she exclaimed,
'What! You don't like the other one?'

JEWISH JOKE

Emotional blockages, as discussed in the previous chapter, are often self-inflicted, albeit unintentionally. In some situations, however, they derive from deliberate manipulation aimed at gaining control. This chapter looks at the prime example of this – emotional blackmail – and examines how the power and control we exert or concede determines our happiness.

A healthy relationship is one where each person respects the needs of the other. Personal values, opinions and attitudes are also respected, even if not agreed upon. When emotional blackmail enters a relationship, honesty disappears and emotional manipulation is used to gain control.

Emotions can provide a powerful force in helping us enjoy life, but they can also be our Achilles heel, allowing us to be vulnerable to the abuse of others. Too often I hear complaints from clients that their relationships are causing them pain, confusion and anger as they succumb to this vulnerability.

'I don't know which way to turn. I figure it out clearly in my mind, but when we discuss it I am always wrong.'

'Somehow I always end up feeling guilty when I suggest something I would like to do.'
'Whenever we have an important discussion I get a terrible
knot in my stomach when he gives his point of view.'

These comments hint at the likelihood that emotional blackmail
is at work, causing confusion, guilt or fear. These emotions
distort the situation or our perception of it and allow the blackmailer to gain or maintain control.

How Emotional Blackmail Works

The dictionary definition of blackmail is 'The exertion of threats
to influence someone or extort payments'. The message from the
blackmailer is, 'Do what I want or you will suffer', and the tools
of enforcement are violence or exposure.

Emotional blackmail involves a similar process but the
enforcement is moral pressure: 'Do what I want or you will feel
bad about going against me'.

Emotional blackmail ranges from the trivial – 'While you are
up, can you get me a cup of tea? I'd do that for you if I was up.'
– to the crippling – 'Do this for me or I will kill myself.'

Case History

Rebecca was a Jewish girl who had fallen in love with a
Catholic boy. Her family were very much against the relationship and used every kind of pressure to break it up, with no
success.

As a last resort they got Rebecca's ailing 80-year-old grand-
mother to exert emotional blackmail. 'I'm not feeling well.
Your relationship is making me ill. If I die, it will be your
fault. Please stop seeing him for my sake if nothing else. You
will be making an old woman very happy.'

Rebecca had no option, the stakes were too high, so she
stopped seeing her beloved.

Control is at the root of all emotional blackmail: one wants it and the other fears resisting. Let's look at a few examples.

Mother to daughter:
'If you really loved me, you wouldn't wear that dress.'

Father to son:
'If you fail your exams, you'll be letting down the family.'

Husband to wife:
'How selfish can you get! All I'm asking is one little favour and you have the audacity to deny me.'

Wife to husband:
'If you were a proper husband, you'd provide for me like my first husband did.'

Boss to worker:
'I've got a terrible headache and it's all your fault because you came to work late this morning.'

The most common emotions used for leverage are fear, guilt and shame. The blackmailer uses unfair tactics to trigger these emotions in the victim and prevent disagreement, thus maintaining control. The manipulation can take different forms – words, facial expressions or actions – but from experience the manipulator knows which methods work best to give them control.

Victims are assailed by emotions that drain confidence and confuse, making it difficult to oppose the blackmailer. 'I know logically what I should do, but I'm so overwhelmed that I become paralysed and just agree to whatever he wants.'

The Blackmailer/Victim Relationship

In order to learn more about this destructive way of relating, we need to look at how the blackmailer and the victim are tied together in the dysfunctional game of emotional blackmail.

To simplify matters I will refer to the blackmailer as 'he' and the victim as 'she'. This does not mean that the majority of black-mailers are male: in fact women are just as likely to play emotional games that give them control over partners or children.

The blackmailer

Like a bully, the blackmailer must get what he wants at all costs. He is egocentric, focused solely on *his* needs, and feels deprived if these are not achieved. He shows no respect for the needs of others and appears to have no interest in their feelings.

Previous relationships have helped him to realise the power of emotional manipulation, and his internal radar detects any vulnerability in his partner. There is an underlying lack of self-esteem that directs him to use blame, anger and guilt as weapons of control. Blaming others helps reduce his own feelings of inadequacy; aggressive outbursts and accusations help him to feel more powerful and nullify his low self-esteem; and inducing guilt allows him to feel superior.

Blackmailers succeed mainly by keeping communication in the emotional arena: any attempt to bring reason to the fore are ignored. Facts are twisted out of all recognition and countered with criticism, blame and judgement: 'How could you be so selfish? How could you do that to me when you know how miserable I feel? You can't love me if you talk that way.'

This line of attack overcomes any resistance by creating guilt and fear. Thus the blackmailer retains his power and the victim remains subservient. 'If I stand up to him/disagree/ignore his bidding he may leave and I couldn't bear that.'

Blackmailers view their opinions and actions as 'positive' and any differing view is regarded as 'negative'. For example, 'I only play golf every weekend to be like other healthy, successful men. You don't like it because you want me to be a wimp and do house-hold chores.' (What I want is right and what you want is wrong.)

The experienced emotional blackmailer uses a variety of techniques to achieve his aims. Sometimes other people are cited to verify his point of view: 'What will people think if you do that?' or 'My friend Bob says you're selfish to go out with your girl-friends on Friday.'

Sometimes the victim is labelled as mad or bad if their views don't coincide with the blackmailer's: 'You're crazy to go line dancing with a lot of old hags. It's only idiots with nothing better to do who go line dancing.'

Comparing the victim negatively to others is also a powerful tool in the blackmailer's armoury: 'Look at Deborah – she doesn't rush to the divorce courts every time her husband has a little fling.'

Words such as 'should', 'must' and 'have to' are used to apply pressure but often without logic: 'You should be going out to work instead of lazing around at home looking after the twins.'

For these techniques to be effective, both blackmailer and victim have to play roles that dovetail into each other. As explained by Dr Susan Forward in her book *Emotional Blackmail*, this interaction relies on the blackmailer enveloping the victim in a fog of confusion that lowers resistance. This fog has three elements:

F = Fear
O = Obligation
G = Guilt

The fog prevents the victim from seeing the blackmailer's actions, threats and attitudes in a realistic light. The confusion he creates prevents her thinking clearly.

Case History

Patsy's father was an unpleasant man by any standards. He had berated and belittled her since she was a child, and to avoid further misery she left home at 17 to make her own way in the world.

When she consulted me she was 25 and married with a baby son. She was having difficulties coping with her father's unheralded appearances at her home.

'My husband and I discuss it all the time but we can never find an answer. We don't like him visiting, especially unannounced, but when we hint at this he goes off the deep end and accuses me of being a terrible daughter.'

Patsy's father used remarks such as, 'How could you say that to me?', 'Your sister is happy any time I visit her', 'Don't forget I'm your father' and 'Do you want your son to grow up without knowing his grandfather?'

Patsy felt overwhelmed whenever her father came to visit. She lost the courage to make a stand, be assertive or enforce her needs. To help her we discussed at length the concept of emotional blackmail, the tactics used by her father and ways for her to relinquish the victim role.

The victim

For a blackmailer to succeed there must be a victim, someone who will 'play the game' and not object. The victim, in effect, *allows* the blackmailer to use emotional manipulation to fulfil his needs. If the threats, criticism and blame fall on deaf ears, the blackmailer will need to change or move on.

It is interesting to note that the victim shares one of the blackmailer's characteristics. She too has a lack of confidence in the area where she is being manipulated; she may be full of self-esteem in other areas, but loses it when the blackmailer 'presses her buttons'.

The victim focuses on the feelings of others and regards them as being of more value than her own, a fact the blackmailer is quick to use for his own ends. She believes she is bad, even wrong, if she doesn't give in to his demands or see things his way. Her emotional pool holds experiences where she felt wrong, hurt, guilty or frightened, and these are triggered by the blackmailer to his advantage.

Some victims could be described as approval addicts: their self-esteem depends on receiving praise from others, so they become vulnerable to manipulation. The blackmailer makes use of this tendency by withholding approval, sulking and withdrawing until he gets his way: 'I just can't stand it when he sulks. The pain and depression are so great I just *have* to give in, then he is all smiles and I feel better.'

The victim becomes like a puppet, her moods depending on which strings are pulled by the blackmailer. He can lift her up with praise or crush her with criticism. She is helpless to make her own moves because her dependency removes her options. She is forever vulnerable to the carrot and stick technique used to drive her in the direction he wants.

Carrot: 'You are such a wonderful person when you do that for me. No wonder I adore you.'

Stick: My first wife always did that for me. Why can't you be like her? It's only a small favour, after all.'

Some victims have a core belief, 'Anything for a peaceful life', that prevents them from saying or doing anything that may disturb the status quo. They take it upon themselves to be the custodian of calm whatever the blackmailer's actions. They are always on edge in case an argument, disagreement or upset occurs, and this attitude gives great scope to the blackmailer as he knows his partner will give in rather than lose the peace.

Some victims take the blame for any problems arising in the relationship. The accusation 'It's all your fault', for example, triggers a response from the emotional pool resulting in defensive apologies.

Case History

Alison was forever being pushed around by her husband. Everything she did was wrong, and these words. 'It's all your fault' were constantly heard in their household. She never argued and somehow managed to feel guilty in spite of a faint intuitive belief that she was not in the wrong.

Her emotional pool contained an important incident that occurred when she was ten. She was watching television when her father entered the room and started changing the channels. An argument followed and in a tantrum she screamed, 'I wish you were dead'. Two days later he died of a massive heart attack and Alison was unable to forgive herself. She carried this guilt with her wherever she went and whatever she did. When her husband blamed her for mistakes, sadness and guilt overwhelmed her, weighing her down further so that she was unable to assert herself.

Alison's therapy took a long time because the guilt was deeply embedded, but she gradually managed to let it go and regain some of the confidence that was rightfully hers.

Some victims have fear of authority figures. They have been bullied by parents or teachers and this fear remains in the emotional pool, eventually being projected on to bosses and husbands. They become children again when the authority figure uses a certain facial expression, tone of voice or action similar to those experienced in childhood. In effect, they relinquish control, applying distorted logic to deal with the situation:

'It's not his fault. He had a terrible upbringing and is really not responsible for his behaviour.'

'He really doesn't mean it.'

'The fact that he hits me proves he loves me. If he didn't care, he wouldn't bother.'

'He is so sensitive. I can take the pain more easily than he can.'

'I know he has a short fuse, but he gets over it so quickly that it really doesn't matter.'

'He doesn't hit me *that* much, only occasionally, and I suppose I deserve it.'

This tactic allows the victim to avoid the facts and steer clear of confrontation and its horrific consequences.

Demand and Ransom

In the standard blackmail situation there is a demand for money in return for a hostage or incriminating information. The consequences of non-payment are physical violence or exposure.

In emotional blackmail the demand is for a particular response to certain behaviour. 'If you don't do what I want, you will suffer emotionally.' The means by which this suffering is caused include threats of leaving, withdrawal of praise, violent outbursts, accusations and criticism: 'You're a hopeless mother. I wish I'd never met you.'

The price paid by the victim is subservience: she must do the blackmailer's bidding without question. This price is very high, causing loss of identity and self-esteem.

Case History

Belinda came to see me because she was having trouble with her partner, Simon. On listening to her story it became obvious Simon was using emotional blackmail to the extreme. I gave her this chapter to read.

She returned one week later saying that she was very confused. Simon had read the chapter and told her that *she* was the emotional blackmailer and *he* was the victim – and she believed him. Once again, he was using emotional blackmail to defend his behaviour and she was again taking on the victim's role!

Breaking Free from Blackmail

Just as being in a relationship with an emotional blackmailer has a price, so regaining control comes at a cost. Blackmailer and victim are bound together by numerous emotional hooks, and breaking free of them can be difficult.

Step 1

As with so many emotional dilemmas, the first step is to be aware of what's going on. The victim must think about what the black-mailer is doing, how she herself is feeling, the emotional manipulation involved and the outcome of their joint behaviour.

Awareness comes from questioning, being alert to messages you are receiving and analysing your internal response. Awareness of the emotions triggered is of prime importance. Learning what they are and resolving them is the first step in overcoming the victim's role. It is important to do this because even if you leave, you will take this vulnerability to the next relationship.

Step 2

Feelings are registered in the body, so being aware of bodily sensations will give you clues as to how the relationship is affecting you.

- Tension in the jaw indicates anger and blocked feelings.
- Tightness in the neck indicates tension, anxiety and stress.
- Hunched shoulders indicate helplessness and guilt.
- Palpitations or tightness in the chest indicate anxiety and fear.

Don't be tempted to ignore or dismiss these sensations – they're important emotional messages.

Step 3

Be aware of what you are telling yourself. Core beliefs and nega-tive self-talk have a major influence in maintaining the victim's role.

- 'It's no big deal: giving in on this little thing won't make any difference.'

- 'What does it matter if I'm uncomfortable as long as he is happy?'
- 'If I love him, that means I'm responsible for his happiness.'
- 'It would be really selfish if I did what *I* want.'

By being aware of your response and what you are telling yourself you can start to influence your actions and reactions.

Step 4

Be aware of the triggers that make you feel bad, guilty, ashamed, frightened or at fault.

- Outbursts of anger
- Blaming accusations
- Bullying tactics and name calling
- Sulking or withdrawal
- Door slamming and storming out

By being aware of these things, you are learning about the blackmailer's methods and the weapons he uses to gain control. Learning the 'game' and how he plays it gives you the strength to stop responding in a loser's way.

Step 5

Be aware of your own responses. A useful technique to help you put your behaviour into perspective is called dissociation. Imagine floating up to the ceiling, then looking down on yourself to see the responses you make to the blackmailer, his reaction and the outcome. Viewing the scenario from a distance allows your rational thoughts to come into play and will help you to devise more effective ways of dealing with his behaviour.

Try the following sequence, filling in the gaps as appropriate. Say to yourself, 'When he says/does *that* I feel *this*.'

This describes the interactions that are occurring between the two of you and enables you to be aware of the emotions caused by his triggers. By repeating this formula whenever a negative emotion occurs, you will begin to understand the mechanism of emotional blackmail.

Say the same thing to the blackmailer: 'Whenever you say/do *that* I feel *this*.'

It is likely he will respond with further accusations, such as 'You've completely misunderstood what I said – you always do' or 'You've been seeing that shrink too much' or 'Your feelings are hopeless, they always get it wrong and screw you up for no reason at all.'

If he doesn't join you in learning about problems in the relationship, you must decide if you wish to stay with him or leave. Both options pose difficulties. If you decide to stay, you will need to learn techniques (see chapter 6) to help you build emotional strength, logic and confidence.

Step 6

Allow each person to take responsibility for their own actions, attitudes and emotions. Too often the victim shoulders responsibility for everything that occurs in the relationship, including the emotions of the other person. By letting them feel sad, angry or frightened and not stepping in to fix it, you are allowing them to grow and learn from the experience. It is not necessary to be a fixer all the time, especially where emotions are involved.

Taking responsibility for your own emotions means that you learn to respond in a more appropriate way when your 'strings are pulled'. You can also learn *not* to respond to the string-pulling and move only of your own accord.

Step 7

Be aware that it takes time to overcome the stranglehold of emotional blackmail. The outcome needs to be some form of change that provides an improvement in or cessation of the relationship. It can take months or even years to adjust to the new circumstances, especially if you choose to leave the 'bad' relationship. In some cases, such as parent and child, leaving is very difficult. Many people simply dilute the relationship by moving abroad and putting some distance between the warring factions. Parent/child bonds are such that complete severance rarely happens.

If change is to occur within the relationship, much work is required by both partners. The blackmailer needs to learn that his partner's feelings and attitudes are as valid as his. He must overcome the fear of not having it all his own way and learn alternative ways of stating his case.

The victim must also learn a great deal – to respect her needs and value her opinions, to stop feeling responsible for everything in the relationship, to stop trying to fix everything and to state her needs without fear or guilt. The aim is to develop honest, adult-to-adult communication that does not involve manipulation or negative emotions.

Staying or leaving both require effort to improve the relationship and prevent negative situations repeating themselves again and again. Learning from experience provides the knowledge and strength to act differently, to notice when emotional blackmail is starting to happen and to deal with it before it takes hold.

15

Improving Emotional Patterns

'Relationships could be better assessed not by the ability to avoid
arguments, but by the ability to resolve them.'

BRIAN ROET

The most common difficulty expressed by couples is that
misunderstandings occur, which escalate into a row or worse. A
crescendo of disagreement can arise from even the most trivial
incident, fuelled by misinterpretation and misunderstanding on
either side.

'Why don't you ever put the cap back on the toothpaste?'
'Leave me alone, you're always picking on me. You're just like
your mother – she always gave your father a really hard time!'
'How dare you bring my mother into this! Your mother wasn't
so great the way she mollycoddled you.'
'All I said was, "Why don't you put the cap on the toothpaste?"
and you explode into a frenzy of vitriol!'
'You haven't heard anything yet if you call that vitriol. What
about the time you . . .'

The spiral of antagonism and anger races forever upwards,
propelled by misunderstanding, hidden agendas, repressed
emotions and past experiences. Every component of the
exchange seems to spark off a more vigorous reply, pouring more
fuel on the fire.

We have all experienced these situations, but for some people
they are the main form of communication: everything ends in

a slanging match. The outcome is not what we want, but it is what we get. One heated comment leads to another, and the situation boils over.

Questioning the process to discover what mechanisms are maintaining these emotional patterns will shed light on alternative and preferable pathways. Let's break the argument about the toothpaste cap into its component parts.

1. The toothpaste cap is obviously not the real bone of contention: it merely triggers the opportunity to air other differences of opinion.
2. Each person is harbouring feelings about the other that, like a landmine, are simply waiting for an opportunity to explode.
3. Emotional baggage, earlier experiences, conflicting viewpoints and lack of acceptance are really the subjects needing discussing.
4. The ammunition used consists of stored hurts and grievances that rise to the surface as the exchange escalates.
5. Differences between the two partners are characterised as wrong or bad rather than just differences. As we all had a unique childhood and upbringing, our attitudes and values may be different, but this doesn't make them wrong or right. Understanding where the other person is coming from is a much better approach than thinking 'If I were them, I would do/think/feel this way'.
6. The energy that propels the argument is coming from emotion not reason. Using pseudo-reason to resolve the conflict simply makes it go round in circles. We need to discuss how we feel.

In any argument it is important to remember that two people can have completely opposite views and both be correct. Many arguments are caused by trying to convince another person that our point of view is correct, when theirs is equally valid. Remember too that resolution will only take place after the battle has subsided. Trying to create rational discussion in the heat of an argument is unlikely to be of any benefit.

Now let's look at the emotions that may be fuelling the argument.

He thinks:

> 'I resent the way she tells me what to do all the time.'
> 'I'm anxious she may turn out like her mother: her father was a cowed and broken man.'
> 'I work hard all day, being lectured to by my boss. I come home for peace and quiet and it starts all over again.'
> 'She wasn't like this when we were first married. She seems to have changed since the kids arrived.'
> 'She never praises or appreciates all the things I do around the house, all she does is notice what I don't do.'

She thinks:

> 'I spend my life tidying up in this house and he can't even bother to put the top on the toothpaste.'
> 'He knows the children will make a mess if the top isn't on, and who will clean it up? Me!'
> 'Why doesn't he realise that I do boring housework all day while he has an interesting job? I feel exhausted and unattractive all the time. He never pays me compliments. Our love life has deteriorated over the last few years, and it makes me really frustrated.'
> 'I know Mum used to give Dad a hard time and I'm terrified I will turn out like her.'

It becomes obvious on analysis that these thoughts and feelings have to be discussed in calmer waters if emotional patterns are to be improved. In order for this to occur three requirements need to be in place.

- Recognition by both parties that they want to improve the relationship and diminish the heated outbursts.
- Agreement by both parties to put aside time and effort to achieve this aim.

• Movitation by both parties to make a change.

Once these three requirements have been agreed, the process of negotiation and conciliation can begin. It is important to realise that harmony will not be achieved by attempting discussions while the argument rages and bullets whistle over head, so declare a truce, make some quiet time to be calm and rational. This needs to be arranged on a regular basis to discuss any conflicts that may have occurred. This process allows one partner to talk and the other to listen. Talking and listening are the two most powerful ingredients for resolution, and certain steps must be followed to allow the process to flow.

The Talking/Listening Process

One partner talks, expressing his or her views about the argu-ments without accusing, criticising or judging. The essential format is, 'When you say/do that, I feel this.' It is an explana-tion of how feelings arose. They don't need to be logical, rational or practical – they are just feelings.

This needs to be accompanied by statements such as, 'When you looked at me that way it reminded me of . . . and I felt . . .' or 'I'd had a dreadful day with the children and was hoping you would help or give me a cuddle when you came home, but you went straight to the TV and turned on the football and I felt . . .'

The other partner listens, making no comment. He doesn't challenge or offer a point of view – he listens, *really* listens, and acknowledges that he has heard by nodding and being attentive. This is not a sign that he agrees or disagrees: it simply shows that he has heard what she said.

This process allows the talker to express her emotions, thoughts and attitudes without being judged or being fearful of the conse-quences, and it lets her know she has got her message across.

After she has said her piece, it is his turn to talk and hers to listen. Again, he is not to judge or criticise but to put his point of view. He can say what it was like for him during the argument, tell her how he felt and what was on his mind.

She is to listen, really listen, not prepare defence arguments while he is talking so that she can reply when he finishes. The aim is to be heard, not to be the victor in an argument.

The acknowledgement 'I heard what you said, I understand how you felt, I see where you were coming from' allows recognition of each other's point of view. The partners may or may not agree, but that is not relevant to this process. It is about being heard and understood.

Time to Reflect

Before the two partners have this 'truce discussion' they may need quiet time on their own to reflect about what happened and what was going on in their mind/body system during the argument. This quiet time enables knotted feelings and misconceptions to be unravelled so that clarity is achieved. During this solitary quiet time it is useful to question what has occurred.

Quiet Time Questions

- 'What happened to me that triggered my response?'
- 'What feelings arose and what thoughts did I have?'
- 'What episodes in my past may have been relevant?'
- 'When have I reacted in a similar way?'
- 'Was it his/her action, facial expressions or what he/she said, that started the process?'
- 'How would I like to react differently if it happened again? What thoughts and feelings would I like to have?'
- 'How much blame, resentment and accusation were involved in my response?'
- 'What did I want to achieve by my attitude?'

- 'Who was I like? Does my action remind me of anyone?'
- 'How could I relinquish my role of "prosecuting lawyer" towards my partner, and take up the role of "defence lawyer"?

Each partner may ask some of these questions of themselves during their personal quiet time *bravery* is necessary to be vulnerable enough to express how you feel; *trust* is another component that allows this vulnerability. Being honest with yourself means that you are able to be open about what you say. *Respecting* each other's feelings is the drop of oil that allows the process to run smoothly.

What Triggers Arguments?

In an American research clinic, children who had temper tantrums were investigated by psychologists, who filmed inter-actions between mothers and children. One camera was focused on the child, another on the mother. When the child had a tantrum or excessive reaction, the psychologist studied the film of the mother's face. On many occasions a brief facial expression occurred that could have represented anger or aggression. On questioning, the mother had no memory of either the facial expression or the emotion.

The team concluded that many of the children's outbursts were related to subliminal messages they were receiving from their mother. The signal, however fleeting, triggered memories of past experiences in the child where anger was appropriate.

Such processes may well occur in arguments between part-ners. The tone of voice, words used, actions, facial expressions or attitudes may trigger memories of the past when emotional pain occurred. Subliminal messages sent by one partner are picked up and acted upon by the other. Neither may be aware this process is happening until the calm discussion at a later time. Often partners learn about specific 'buttons' that can be pressed to create a response. In the discussion about the tooth-paste cap, for example, the accusation 'You're just like your mother' is such a button. In the discussions during the truce time such comments should be pointed out so that each partner can avoid sensitive areas in the future.

Resolving Arguments

Humour is a great balm in emotional conflicts. The ability to see the funny side helps put the argument into perspective and provide resolution.

Case History

Steve and Liz were a happily married couple who discussed their ability to resolve marital arguments in a seminar I was running.

Steve said, 'We have a saying: "Keep the milk cold", which helps to make light of a situation if we are getting too serious and niggly with each other. Some years ago we had heated arguments about milk being left out of the fridge. Liz believed it didn't matter as it would be drunk by the family before it went off, but I said it should always be returned to the fridge because I hated making tea with sour milk.

'We set up an experiment to determine who was right, leaving milk out for different lengths of time, but in the end it was hopeless. We couldn't come to any conclusion and finished rolling about with laughter at our experiment and the triviality of our argument.

'Ever since then, if one of us says "Keep the milk cold" when we are building up a head of steam, we both burst out laughing at the memory those words bring. The laughter puts things into perspective and changes our mood instantaneously.'

Resolving emotional conflicts can also be helped by non-verbal communication. Sitting quietly together, cuddling or holding hands all have a role in carrying positive messages from one to the other.

Saying sorry is often very difficult, but it has a powerful effect in reducing anger. Partners often complain more about the lack of apology than the original wound. The boxer Mike Tyson, for example, spent three years in jail after being found guilty of rape because he couldn't say sorry. His victim said she would not have pressed charges if he had apologised. Tyson evidently found it easier to spend three years in jail than say sorry.

Saying 'sorry' is often very difficult.

The majority of arguments between couples are emotionally driven, but if you follow the guidelines in this chapter emotional outbursts will become a thing of the past.

16

The Power of Words

'Sticks and stones may break my bones but words will never hurt me.'
PROVERB

Words are the main carriers of information, but they often prove to be an inadequate way of communicating: the message given is not the one received. This chapter looks at the role of words in emotional communication and suggests ways in which they can be used more effectively.

Imagine you are in a cinema absorbed in the film when someone shouts 'Fire'. Pandemonium and chaos would certainly result even if there were no fire. This shows that we *are* affected by words and that there is a direct connection between the words we hear and emotions that result. The pain may not be physical, as with sticks and stones, but it is real and upsetting.

Words that Wound

If someone calls us 'stupid', a 'liar' or a 'cheat', we are affected emotionally by the accusation. We may feel hurt, ashamed, guilty or angry in response to the words and tone of voice.

The intensity of the emotion depends on many factors – the person who spoke, the situation involved, and the self-belief of the person accused. If we haven't lied, our response may be one of indignation or anger. If we lack confidence, we may feel fear or guilt, even though the accusation is false.

Case History

Molly, an anxious client of mine, was referred to a specialist for some tests related to abdominal symptoms. She came to see me in a state of panic.

'I'm terrified about the results of those tests,' she said.

'Have you seen the specialist?' I asked.

'Yes, and he said the tests were "pretty good".'

'That must have been reassuring,' I replied.

'No, quite the reverse. It's made me really concerned there is something wrong. He said "pretty good", but if the tests were normal, he would have said "very good".'

I suggested that I ring the specialist's secretary straight away and resolve the matter. Molly agreed, and the specialist's secretary confirmed that the tests were normal.

'I'm so relieved,' she said after the phone call. 'I haven't slept for nights because I was so worried about what he meant by "pretty good".'

The way we respond to situations depends a great deal on our state of mind at the time. For example, a fluttering bedroom curtain seen in daylight when we are feeling calm might provoke the response, 'It's just the wind'. That same curtain seen at night when we are alone and nervous might make us think 'What if it's a burglar'.

It's just the same with verbal messages. We may hear words that are not said, miss words that *are* spoken, or distort them to create miscommunication. Molly's anxiety had made her interpret positive words in a negative way.

Case History

David is very good at his work but he has a low opinion of himself. He learnt in childhood from parental comments that he was lazy, stupid and would never succeed.

This was far from the truth, but because David had heard it so often, he believed it to be the case. Whenever anyone praised him at work he felt they must be joking, being sarcastic, didn't know what they were talking about, or wanted a favour. Words spoken in all honesty were twisted beyond recognition to maintain his low self-esteem. Because *he* thought so little of himself, he couldn't believe anyone else could think otherwise.

The people whose words have the most effect on our feelings are those close to us – family, friends, colleagues or employers. Authority figures may well influence us in a similar manner to our parents. In order to diminish our response to words, we need to learn how to protect ourselves from them. By building self-confidence and feeling that we are normal, healthy adults, we can shrug off the admonishments, criticism and abuse that comes our way.

Words that Trigger

In childhood, millions of words are directed at us by parents, teachers and classmates. Many of these words cause emotions, which are stored in our emotional pool. Pleasant experiences, such as love, care and support, will form a positive emotional pool and an optimistic outlook. Unpleasant experiences, such as shame, guilt and fear, will create a negative emotional pool and a pessimistic outlook.

When emotive words are spoken in adulthood, a response is triggered from the emotional pool that makes us feel the way we felt in childhood. These stored feelings are more powerful than logic and can make us over-react. Emotions are more powerful than logic, and when both are triggered it is the emotion that will take control.

When I was young my mother often called me 'stupid' and a

'fool', and these words still have a powerful effect on me.

I recall one hot summer day when I was ten – we were out for a drive, and I was sitting in the back seat wearing a jumper. After a little while my mother turned around and said, 'Brian, aren't you hot in that jumper?'

'No, Mum, I'm fine,' I replied.

We drove on, then she turned around again and said, 'You must be hot, Brian. It's boiling outside.'

'No, Mum, I feel OK,' I again replied.

A little later she again turned around, 'Brian, it's the middle of summer: how can you stand to wear a jumper in this heat?'

'I'm really feeling OK, Mum.'

Finally, she turned around and said, 'You're a fool to wear that jumper. Take it off – you're making me feel hot.'

Reluctantly, I did as she told me, conscious that the jumper had ruined our Sunday drive.

My mother's comments have been stored in my emotional pool for all my adult life. If someone calls me stupid, even in jest, I can feel the emotion well up, despite my conscious awareness that I am not stupid.

After I graduated in medicine I remember thinking, 'I'm a doctor, yet I'm constantly labelled as stupid. How can this be?'

If my mother were still alive, I could imagine her saying to me, 'Brian, you're a fool. You know I didn't really mean you were stupid.'

Self-talk

Most people have a constant internal dialogue with themselves – a continuous commentary on their thoughts, actions, beliefs and feelings. This self-talk varies from person to person, but always plays a major role in how we feel and in forming our attitudes and beliefs.

Past worriers would use words such as 'If only –' and create self-blame.

Future worriers would use 'What if –?' to create anxiety and concern.

Punishers would say, 'I shouldn't have done that', 'It's all my fault', 'I don't deserve to succeed' to create guilt.

Critics would say, 'How could you have missed that opportunity?' to create low self-esteem.

Judges would say, 'Why can't you do as well as your father did?' to create low self-worth.

All these characters live in our mind and influence emotions by their utterances. They don't need to make logical sense to upset us – they just need to say the words and feelings will overwhelm us. There is a direct connection between the words we tell ourselves and the way we feel.

It follows that if we can change our self-talk from accusing and blaming to accepting and praising, we have a powerful tool to change our emotions from fear and guilt to calmness and confidence. Look at the following to see how you can alter your internal vocabulary to achieve a more positive outcome.

If we change our self-talk, we can change our emotional response.

Changing negative to positive

- 'Should', 'must', 'ought' (and 'shouldn't', 'mustn't', 'oughtn't') are words that imply someone else (in our minds) is telling us what to do. By changing these words to 'I will', 'I am going to', 'I choose to', *we* are making the decision and are in control.
- 'I'm a failure' or 'I'm hopeless' are both untrue and unhelpful. Telling yourself 'I accept myself as I am (for the time being)' lessens the load and allows you to achieve your potential without the weight of self-criticism.

    Similarly, avoid judging yourself in terms of success/ failure, right/wrong, good/bad, and ask yourself 'What have I learnt from that experience?'
- 'It's my fault' is uttered by people who have a victim mentality, always feeling guilty and taking the blame. It is preferable to realise that circumstances are often nobody's fault. Tell yourself instead, 'I'm doing the best I can'.
- 'Try' is a word that can imply failure. For example, saying 'I'll try to climb that wall' implies that you feel doubtful of succeeding. Your chances of success will be greater if you say 'I will do that' or 'I am going to do that'.
- 'It's vital' is a statement that puts us under a lot of pressure. In reality, most things are not so important that we should risk our well-being for them, and reflection after the event often shows the truth of this. Telling yourself 'It really doesn't matter' allows you to perform with much less pressure, and perhaps with more success.
- 'They make me feel –' is a victim's attitude that gives power to others, allowing them to control your emotions. Saying instead, 'I *allow* them to make me feel –' focuses on *your* role in the situation and makes you think about ways of not allowing them to manipulate your feelings.
- 'I'm feeling not too bad' is a negative way of saying something positive, namely 'I feel good'. Similarly, telling someone 'You have nothing to fear' is less reassuring than 'You are safe'. With the 'negative' statements the unconscious

mind latches onto the negative words, 'bad' and 'fear', so the positive message does not get through. The answer is to avoid these negative turns of speech, which therapists call 'double negatives', and use simple positive statements instead.

- 'Need' is a powerful word. It conveys the idea that something is essential and that we have no choice in the matter. Using the words 'want', 'desire' or 'wish' instead removes the sense of compulsion and reduces the pressure we place on ourselves.
- 'Problem' has negative connotations suggesting a difficulty that must be tackled, and that will be a burden on our energy and emotions. Using the word 'nuisance' instead produces a different response. A nuisance is annoying but does not place demands on us – we can live with it.
- 'But' is a word that blocks and negates what has just been said. It stops the flow of thought like a brick wall. Using 'and' instead allows thoughts and conversation to flow more freely.
- 'Confrontation' implies conflict and unpleasantness, so it sends many people into avoidance mode. Changing it to 'negotiation' suggests flexibility and control, and makes the situation less frightening.

If we are to achieve our potential, our internal dialogue should be positive and self-praising rather than critical. Emotions need to be protected, just as children do. People who are hard on themselves, making critical and derogatory remarks both internally and externally, make life very difficult for themselves. Life is difficult enough without the added burden of self-criticism.

Use the power of words in a positive way, like nourishing a plant and allowing it to grow strong and productive. Tell yourself you are doing the best you can, and you will do better and feel better.

Remember, a tree can make a million matches and one match can burn a million trees.

External Messages

Every day we are bombarded with messages – some from the people in our lives, some from radio, television and newspapers. All these messages will, to some extent, be coloured by the person or source from which they emanate. For example, a worrier will have a different perspective from a pragmatist, and tabloid newspapers will report stories very differently from the broadsheets.

In these cases the messengers may not be conscious of conveying their hidden agenda. Such is not the case, though, with the advertising industry, which uses words deliberately to manipulate the thoughts and emotions of prospective purchasers. 'Farm fresh eggs', for example, conveys wholesomeness and naturalness, distracting thoughts from the battery conditions where the eggs were probably produced. Advertisers know that shopping is often an emotional procedure, so they use words to trigger feelings that will make the customer more likely to buy.

The lesson we can learn from this is not only to listen to what people say, but also to be aware of who is saying it. We cannot prevent others using words in a manipulative way, but we can protect ourselves from them.

Take note of the French prayer: 'Oh God, may my words be gentle today for tomorrow I may have to eat them.'

PART ·III

Techniques to Help
Emotional Balance

17

The Therapeutic Process

'Listen and you will hear; hear and you will see;
see and you will feel; feel and you will know.'

BRIAN ROET

During the last session of a client's therapy, I ask what has helped
them to overcome their problem. More often than not, they look
at the ceiling, and ponder for a little while, then reply: 'I think
it was having someone to listen to me.'

What is this thing called listening and why is it so powerful
in helping people with emotional problems? Why do people need
to visit a stranger and pay for what seems a normal component
of everyday communication?

In order to answer these questions, it's necessary to look at
what happens between client and therapist that aids emotional
resolution.

Who Seeks Help?

People who seek therapy, like those who enter a bookshop on a
rainy day, fall into three categories.

Visitors are simply sheltering from the rain. They come so that
they can tell themselves and others they don't need help, or
couldn't be helped.
Complainers come to whinge and criticise others. Why aren't

the books they want in stock? Why aren't the booksellers more helpful? It is always someone else's problem, and never their own fault.

Customers come to buy a book. They are aware of their need to change, and are prepared to spend time and effort and take risks in order to do so.

The person who seeks therapy has been likened to someone who has sat on a cactus and has 100 spines in his bottom. Healing doesn't occur spontaneously, so he sees a doctor, who removes three or four spines at each session. The extractions cause pain, but only when all 100 spines are removed will the person feel comfortable again.

Contacting a Therapist

Making the first appointment can be sparked by the suggestion of a doctor, family member or friend, by a book or magazine article, or by symptoms simply becoming unbearable. The important thing is to seek therapy at the right time, which is when it fits in with your needs and motivation.

Making the initial phone call is an acknowledgement that you have a problem and are seeking a solution. If the voice at the other end provides reassurance, confidence, a belief that they can help, then hope and expectations are increased. Hope is an energising companion during the therapeutic journey, and it can start with the initial phone call. It can even help to resolve the problem *before* the client meets the therapist.

Some years ago I was phoned by a woman who needed help to relax in order to become pregnant. She had received fertility treatment over six years without success and her doctor had suggested relaxation to reduce the anxiety that might be adversely affecting her fertility. I arranged to see her in a month's time. During our first consultation I taught her a relaxation technique and suggested that she practise it daily. I made an appointment to see her two weeks later. In the interim she rang to cancel as she was now pregnant. I extolled the virtues of relaxation until she interrupted, saying, 'The relaxation was very nice but in fact I became pregnant between the phone call and the first consultation.'

Was this a complete coincidence? Perhaps the hope she felt following our initial phone conversation allowed her to relax enough to let her reproductive system perform successfully.

Many people become anxious before their first visit. What will the therapist be like? Will he be on my wavelength and understand how I feel? Will he tell me what to do against my wishes? Will it open a can of worms? Will he think I am mad or wasting his time? What if he can't help me?

These and many more questions can cause a heightened emotional state in the client. In fact, sometimes the build-up is so great that they burst into tears soon after meeting me. These tears are a sign of relief that they are able to let go of stored-up emotions that have been heightened by the anxiety of the preceding days.

Clients are genuinely surprised by this sudden release of emotion in front of a complete stranger. They are embarrassed and apologetic, but it is a good sign that they feel safe enough to lower their defences.

Assessing the Therapist

When clients enter the consulting room and meet the therapist they should feel safe – safe to express themselves, safe to be emotional, safe from criticism, blame or judgement. It should be a place different from all others, a place where one hour is going to be completely devoted to their needs. It is their time to focus on themselves, be as selfish as they like, say anything they wish and feel safe to do so – just as a trapeze artist is given confidence by the presence of a safety net.

A client related a consultation she had experienced with another therapist. 'He met me at the door and for some reason I didn't feel comfortable when I saw him. He led me downstairs

The therapist needs to provide a safety net
of support to allow clients to face their fears.

to a consulting room in the basement and locked the door. He asked me to sign a form stating he was not responsible for any mishaps, should they occur. He then tried to reassure me by telling me not to be scared as he wouldn't molest me while I had my eyes closed during hypnosis. I was terrified and couldn't wait to leave.' Hardly a suitable way to build confidence and safety, was it?

It is important for clients to have 'good vibes' about the therapist and consulting room. These vibrations are difficult to describe, but they are real and felt by the client nevertheless. At a deep level we know if we trust someone and are prepared to divulge secrets and fears to them. We know if we can take the risk to say something we've never told anyone else, release a guilty experience, or talk in a manner open to ridicule. It takes courage to do these things, and the environment needs to be suitable for such courage to be transformed into action.

The Client/Therapist Relationship

Through shared, non-judgemental exploration the client can learn about thoughts and feelings that are causing trouble, and devise ways to develop more appropriate ones. Often this involves re-learning what is already known rather than new learning. Clients repeatedly say, 'I already knew what you have told me but somehow I hadn't been aware of it.' At some level, clients generally know everything they need to make the changes they require. They know, but don't know they know. Part of the therapist's work is to help them realise this.

The relationship – between client and therapist has a particular energy that facilitates the process of getting better. The therapist is not a 'fixer' – he is a guide, providing information and support to help clients proceed in the best possible way.

Think of yourself as a garden full of beautiful flowers, shrubs and trees which have been overrun by weeds. The therapist provides you with tools but you still need to do the work of removing the weeds.

Listening

The need to be listened to and heard is fundamental for someone in therapy. Listening is an art rather than a science, a gift rather than a technique. The therapist's ability to listen is the one most often noticed by clients. However, his sensitivity, understanding and knowledge are equally important: they reveal his personality and attitude, which must suit the client or the therapy is doomed.

Attentive listening is not restricted to therapists. Religious leaders, for example, are good listeners, having been trained in pastoral care. But listening just comes naturally to some people. Friends, relatives and colleagues are often willing to lend an ear to our problems and provide a shoulder to cry on. Indeed, the proximity of their support and understanding can make us feel a great deal better when we most need it.

This is amply illustrated by a discovery at an American hospital. It was noticed that patients on a certain ward recovered much more quickly than on others, and the reason was found to be a cleaner called Clara. Every night Clara would sit on the end of each patient's bed listening to their troubles. Although the hospital employed trained counsellors, the patients preferred Clara's homespun philosophy and street-wise nature. They commented that she always had time for them and was never in a hurry to move on.

Inevitably, some people are averse to sharing their feelings with others for fear of being blamed, disbelieved, criticised or re-opening old wounds: 'What's the use of talking about it? It's all water under the bridge and I need to get on with my life.'

Such views are understandable, but experience shows that the Archbishop of Canterbury, Dr Robert Runcie, was correct in his observation following the Hungerford massacre: 'The sharing of hurt is the beginning of healing.'

Trust

When sharing emotions, trust is a most important commodity. It allows us to feel safe and release thoughts or feelings that we would not risk with others. It is instinctive and cannot be switched on at will, as the following story demonstrates.

A little boy was playing on a mountainside when a man approached him.

'I collect wild flowers and there is one I'd really like to have, but it is out of my reach down the mountain. If I give you a pound, will you reach down and get the flower while I hold your feet?'

The little boy thought for a while, then said, 'Mister, I'll fetch my dad: he can hold my feet and I'll get your flowers for nothing.'

People who seek the therapist's counsel do so either because they do not have close friends to rely on, or because they believe their problem is not suitable for the ears of friends. Sometimes it is easier to unburden to a stranger, and it rules out the danger of altering a friendship in a way that both parties might later regret.

The saying 'A problem shared is a problem halved' has much merit, and organisations such as the Samaritans show that many people agree with it. Every year thousands of people benefit from the trained ear at the other end of the telephone. Having someone to talk to helps dispel the fears that grow in the darkest hours of the night, when helplessness is often at its worst.

What Happens in the Consulting Room?

Listening that occurs in normal conversation differs from that in therapy. The therapist gives his complete attention to the client's needs, using all his senses to pick up messages both verbal and physical. Not all these messages are responded to straight away: they may be noticed, then filed away to be utilised at a later time to help the client gain greater awareness and under-standing. Of course, it is very important to notice contradictions between verbal and visual messages: blushing, eye movements, tears and grimaces all give clues to the workings of mind/body systems.

Clients' emotions can vary considerably during a session. They may feel challenged, relieved, hopeful, happy or sad, for example, and all these feelings are useful in understanding what is actu-ally happening inside. The therapist's role is to reflect and interpret, offering rational explanations and appropriate encour-agement to help the client feel as if a weight is being lifted from them.

Early consultations can also be used by the client to assess the suitability of the therapist. Is his response to disclosures helpful and supportive? Do you feel safe in revealing your inner-most thoughts and feelings to him?

As feelings are generally what lead a client to therapy, they are also the main focus of attention during the consultation. The more that is learnt about troublesome feelings, the better the client will feel: expressing them, learning the role they play, understanding their influence and assessing whether or not they are appropriate is the basis of the therapeutic process.

Each session lasts about an hour and can be used in any way the client likes – talking, asking questions, listening, or even sitting in silence. In my opinion, the most important thing we therapists have to offer to our clients is time that has depth as well as length. This quality time is devoted to the client without interruption or distraction. The client can explore, take risks, express feelings and learn to see things differently, all at a pace that they feel comfortable with. The therapist never hurries them.

After the session many of the points discussed will reverberate in the client's mind. The new learning that has occurred needs to be absorbed into the system, and old patterns adjusted to accommodate it. Attitudes and beliefs will probably be questioned, and there may be a new awareness of feelings, responses and perspective. This allows what has been discussed in theory to be put into practice.

Hope

Another major factor in the healing process is hope – a combination of expectation and desire. Its presence can fill us with confidence, while its absence can rob us of purpose and motivation.

Some people fear hope, and do not allow themselves to be hopeful in case their desires are not met. Others regard it as the light at the end of the tunnel: 'It is the hope that I will succeed that keeps me coming for therapy and working on my problems.'

Providing hope during a consultation creates energy for the client to move towards a desired outcome. The therapist can do this in a number of ways, such as noticing progress, praising improvements and being aware of change. Many clients go around in circles when hope is missing. The therapist provides support to prevent this circularity and guides the client away from despair and towards hope. The client's realisation that hope may be fulfilled provides more hope, more energy for the journey into the future. The underlying message is, 'If you continue working on your problem the way you are, you will succeed.'

Homework

Between visits the client is sometimes asked to do 'homework' in order to put the theory discussed into practice. This may involve listening to a tape, reading a book, overcoming a fear or taking a risk. Alternatively, they may be asked to become more aware of the feelings and triggers relating to a particular aspect of their problems. This is learning from experience (experiential learning) and occurs in the real world rather than the artificial world of the consulting room. The client can report back on this, or any other experience, at the next session. 'I was terrified in the supermarket today. I'll mention this at the next consultation and see what I can learn from it.'

Sharing experiences and feeling 'I'm not on my own' are helpful in dealing with the situation, as well as learning from it. On occasion this attitude alone is enough to solve the problem: by the time the next session comes round, time has resolved it.

Motivation

One of the greatest factors in determining the outcome of therapy is motivation. Many people say they will do anything to get better, but constantly fail to do the homework agreed: 'I didn't have time because Granny came to stay'; 'I would have listened to the tape but I didn't have any batteries'; 'I completely forgot what I had agreed to do'; 'I was too tired to read the book you gave me'.

This lack of motivation underlies most of the failures that occur in therapy. It is important to put time and effort into making changes because if these are not forthcoming, the outcome is less than anticipated.

Remember, the therapist does not fix your problem – you do.

18

How to Use Your Intuition

'Intuition is the language of the soul'

NEALE DONALD WALSCH, *CONVERSATIONS WITH GOD*

When I came to write this chapter my first thoughts were whether intuition deserves a place in a book about emotions. I concluded that as we run our lives by thoughts, feelings and intuition, it is reasonable to include intuition in order to understand our behaviour more completely.

The dictionary definition of intuition is 'Immediate insight without conscious reasoning'. This informed me that it is quick and that we don't consciously know about it. However, it didn't actually tell me what intuition is.

It has been said that intuition is like a wild bird entering a room by the window, circling swiftly around, then flying out again after a few seconds. This image adds another grain of information, namely that intuition is fleeting and evanescent. It also suggests that intuition is not connected to logic – coming in the window rather than the door, and that it has a mystical component – arriving from the heavens to visit only briefly.

There are many phrases used to describe intuition, none very exact, but that is its nature. We talk about having a gut reaction, a feeling in the bones, a hunch, a sixth sense and an instinct. None of these are scientific: with intuition we know, but we don't know *how* we know.

'I've just met Graham and I really don't like him.'

'Why? What's wrong with him?'

'I don't know, but there is something about him that makes me feel uncomfortable.'

Intuition is also defined as instinctive knowledge or insight, which suggests that the information is coming from another area of our brain or from our evolutionary past. A combination of instinct and insight (a sudden understanding of a complex situation or problem) is a very powerful force indeed, endowing us with animal cunning and the ability to understand the situation as a whole. This is rather different from other thought processes, which tend to focus on a specific part of the person or situation.

The modern world's high regard for rationality and scientific explanations has seen intuition relegated to a lesser role. Hunches are difficult to explain and harder to prove, so less value is placed on them. Not so in less technologically advanced cultures, where intuition plays a major role in social cohesion.

Intuitive messages are often brief and hard to pin down, so it is only too easy to ignore or disregard them. Judy's case history shows how shortsighted this can be.

Case History

Judy came to seek help because she was distraught about the break-up of her 20-year marriage.

'I'm leaving Jim because I can't cope with his lying. He seems to enjoy telling lies, even when there is no benefit to him. He has problems with the truth. I think he is a pathological liar, and I can't stand it any more.'

'How long have you known about his lying?'

Judy thought for a little while.

'In fact I had a hunch about it in the first week we met. It was nothing serious and I couldn't quite put my finger on it but some part of me suspected it from the start. I loved him and it was such fun being with him, so I pushed it to the back of my mind.'

Judy had been receiving information about Jim via her

intuitive pathway, but for obvious reasons she didn't want to listen. It was only with time, when the message became louder and clearer, that she was forced to take action.

Intuition is a special feeling or thought that differs from normal thoughts and feelings. It can be likened to an inner voice that gives us information at a more subtle level. To understand this, think of the mind/body complex as a radio with many stations, providing a vast array of information and entertainment. As we turn the dial, we receive different messages – our thoughts and our feelings. The 'intuition station' is very soft and requires fine tuning for its messages to be received. It needs quiet so it won't be drowned out, and focused attention to understand what is being said.

In order to make the most use of this station, we need to respect it, trust it and value the information being broadcast. We need to pay attention to the message, as it lasts only a short while and is not repeated. This station is more powerful for some people than for others: these are the intuitive ones.

How Intuitive Are You?

The psychiatrist Carl Jung described four types of personality, but each of us possesses elements of all four.

- Sensation type – establishes that something exists using the senses.
- Thinking type – tells us what it means.
- Feeling type – tells us what its value is.
- Intuitive type – surmises where it comes from and whither it goes. A sixth sense for hidden possibilities.

Our individual personality is labelled according to which of the four types is dominant. Some people are by nature intuitive, and lead their lives largely on this basis. Jung described intuition as 'Outside the province of reason but not necessarily contrary to it'.

We tend to use the most dominant of the four in our character to deal with the world, leaving the others to be less influential. Indeed, the influence of reason often overrides the quiet, fleeting messages of intuition.

Women are considered more intuitive than men, perhaps because they are more in touch with their emotions. Often their intuition is accurate but they don't trust themselves to act on it. When emotional and intuitive feelings act in parallel we have a certainty about our attitude that is otherwise lacking.

It is possible to grade intuitive ability on a scale, just as we can grade height, weight and intelligence. At one end of the scale are those who have a low intuitive capacity. They rely on thoughts and feelings to guide them, and are not tuned into the radio station called intuition. They have the ability to improve this situation but choose not to because they value thoughts or feelings so highly.

In the middle of the scale are people whose intuitive messages blend with thoughts and feelings. They listen to more stations, so they have an increased amount of information to choose from. They value, respect and utilise intuition in many areas, and find it a useful and helpful guide when acknowledged.

At the top end of the scale are sensitive people, such as healers, clairvoyants and psychics. Their intuition is on another level, as they claim to channel information and energy from outside themselves rather than from their own personal experience. In fact, psychic people provide information that could not have come from their personal experience. Carl Jung postulated that they tap into a 'collective unconscious', where they access information outside their personal experience. Clairvoyants and psychics have this ability to a marked degree.

As intuition comes from deep within us, and bases its influence on a total view of our inner needs, it is often in conflict with our intellectual or material requirements. Someone might say, for example: 'My instinct is to leave my job as it just doesn't feel right, but I have the mortgage to pay.' Such conflicts are difficult to resolve because there is often no pathway that satisfies both personal and material needs. The 'internal master' often loses out to the 'external' one.

Where Can Intuition Help You?

There are a number of areas where intuition can play a major role, giving us information unavailable by other means:

- In relationships – helping to assess the other person's character to decide how we can relate to them.
- In decision-making – when alternatives confront us.
- In future events – when we have premonitions about things yet to happen.
- In matters of security – when trying to determine a safe course of action.

In the patchwork quilt that makes up intuition, an important panel relates to our intuitive energy in relationships. Intuitive people 'know' the character of someone they meet, and often their gut feeling is correct. Having this ability and acting on the information provides sound guidelines for a successful relationship.

It may be that part of intuition is the ability to recognise minimal cues – body language or 'vibrations' given off by someone but not received consciously. If this information is processed with other visual or verbal clues, we get the message about someone in a variety of ways and a stronger impression is obtained.

Another aspect of intuition that may be relevant is called pattern recognition. When we have experienced something repeatedly, we store the pattern of experience in our mind/body system. When a new event occurs that is similar to the stored pattern, we recognise it and act accordingly. Our prior knowledge influences us even though we may not be aware what this prior knowledge actually is.

A very intuitive friend of mine, who is also a therapist, told me he often surprises new clients when he makes statements resulting from his pattern recognition. Having seen many clients over the years, he is able to recognise certain behaviours that reveal prior experiences. When he comments, for example, 'You must have been bullied as a child,' or 'Did your father leave home when you were very young?' his new clients are incredulous and suspect him of being clairvoyant.

Improving Your Intuitive Ability

It is said that we are born with a certain level of intuition, some more than others, and by respecting and responding to it we can achieve our full potential. Belief and trust in our intuition sends energy around the mind/body system, giving it more power. If we disbelieve, block, ignore or fail to act on intuitive messages, the energy decreases.

How can we assess how intuitive we actually are? First we need to be aware of the gut reaction or inner voice that occurs in a variety of situations, such as assessing someone's character. Often our intuition will be neither logical nor rational, but it will be insistent.

Once we are aware of this gut reaction, we need to assess its reliability, and only time will tell if your instincts are right. If in doubt, be wary of relying on intuition until it proves itself.

By becoming aware of your intuitive feelings, perhaps noting them down and assessing them at a future date, you can learn about their value and reliability. There is no point in being intuitive if the intuition in incorrect. This constant testing allows you and your intuitive powers to work together to become more accurate and helpful. It's like nourishing a part of yourself that has been neglected. Remember – use it or lose it.

An excellent book by Shakti Gawain called *Developing Intuition* explains in easy steps how to improve your intuitive skills. The method involves awareness, quiet time, meditation and focusing on the messages you receive via special thoughts and feelings. As the messages are subtle, you need to quieten any internal or external interference blocking your intuition. Being in a meditative state allows you to focus on any intuitive messages coming from mind or body.

Be aware that intuition can sometimes be drowned out by emotion, such as when we are overawed by someone's status, madly in love, riddled with guilt or consumed by jealousy. It pays to be alert to this so that we don't make the wrong choices.

To tap into your intuition it can be helpful to think of yourself as being made of many parts. Some parts you enjoy, others you don't. In among them is the intuitive part, and although its voice is not very loud, its value is great. By learning to hear this intuitive part when it is tugging at your sleeve, you are developing a powerful resource that is wise and experienced and knows the whole of you very well.

> Reason is an effort to know the unknown
> and intuition is the happening of the unknowable.
> To penetrate the unknowable is possible,
> but to explain it is not.
> The feeling is possible,
> the explanation is not.
>
> Osho, Indian mystic

19

Quiet Time

'Sometimes doing nothing is doing something
of the utmost importance.'

BRIAN ROET

Following the processes of talking and listening comes the need
for quiet reflection. This chapter deals with that need, which I
believe to be one of the most important components of
emotional equilibrium.

Just as the body's physical requirements – food, water, exercise, rest – all play a role in maintaining health, so its
psychological needs must be met. Emotions also require attention and nourishment in order to serve us in the best possible
manner.

States of Mind

In simple terms, the mind can be considered to operate on three
distinct levels. We pass back and forth between two of these
levels throughout the day, and move to the third at night. Each
of these states is associated with a particular pattern of brain-
waves.

1. **The conscious state – beta rhythm**
    This involves functions such as rational thought, analysis,
    speech and controlled actions. Also known as a 'trying'

Doing nothing is doing something very important.

state of mind, it is an active and aware state with a frequency of 17–25 hertz (cycles per second).

2. **The meditative state – alpha rhythm**

   Also called the trance state, altered state and daydream state, this involves emotional activity, creativity, relaxation and visualisation. This 'being' state of mind is awake and relaxed, 8–12 hertz.

3. **Sleep – delta rhythm**

   This involves relaxation, regeneration and release of different emotional material via dreams. It consists of large-amplitude slow waves, 1–3 hertz.

Emotions can be felt in all three states, but the one I wish to discuss is the meditative state, as it plays a major role in maintaining emotional equilibrium, and is the state of mind involved with what I call 'quiet time'.

Some years ago an American psychologist called Ernest Rossi performed an experiment involving a number of people who stayed in a house where they could not assess time: the windows were blacked out, and clocks, radios and television removed. The occupants had no idea what time it was or whether it was day or night. Electroencephalogram leads were attached to their heads so that their brainwave patterns could be monitored, and they were allowed to do whatever they wished whenever they wished. There was no pressure on them to perform in any way.

After a number of days, when the participants had settled into a routine, it was noticed that they developed a brainwave pattern that followed a specific rhythm during the waking state. This pattern consisted of 90 minutes of alert activity followed by 20 minutes of relaxed activity. Dr Rossi believes this is our natural pattern and called it 'ultradian rhythm'.

In his book *The 20-Minute Break*, Dr Rossi puts forward the theory that this pattern is beneficial for the mind/body complex, and problems arise because we spend too long in the active 'trying' phase, and not enough time in the relaxed 'being' phase. He maintains that the pressure of life prevents us achieving this balanced pattern, which nature intended to be the framework of our lives. Our emotions and the way they influence us are being disturbed by the lack of our 20-minute break.

People who are stressed and have emotions 'all over the place' are operating on beta rhythm. The lack of alpha rhythm causes an imbalance in brain functioning similar to that caused by lack of delta rhythm (sleep), namely tiredness, poor concentration and memory loss.

In everyday life it is not possible to stop every 90 minutes and relax for 20, but it *is* possible to be aware of our needs and make time to move into this relaxed state sometime during the day. This is what I call 'quiet time', a period of alpha-rhythm relaxation.

Our feelings tell us when we need quiet time: tiredness, anxiety and anger, for example, indicate that we need a break, and heeding these messages is the same as nourishing ourselves. This nourishment could be compared to watering a plant – the flowers and leaves are above the surface and the roots under the ground. Nourishing the flowers and leaves will not be nearly as useful as nourishing the roots by watering the soil. Quiet time nourishes our roots allowing us to remain healthy and in balance.

When I ask clients, 'How much time do you spend doing nothing each day?' they usually say something like, 'Not much actually, I'm always so busy. I watch a bit of TV when I get the chance, but I'm generally on the go all the time. I never really have time to relax, there is always so much to do.'

Watching TV may be pleasant and relaxing but it is not genuine quiet time because it is 'doing' rather than 'being', and parts of the mind are still active.

Quiet time occurs when you sit or lie undisturbed on your own with eyes closed, having no aims or agenda – whatever happens is acceptable. You are giving yourself a present – time for yourself. There are many ways to learn about this meditative state, including transcendental meditation, yoga, self-hypnosis, daydreaming, and autogenic training. The goal, however, remains the same – to achieve a level where your mind is quiet, relaxed and tranquil.

Alongside the listening and support that clients get from therapy, I generally advise that they have quiet time each day to enhance whatever other improvements they are making. If they continue to rush around, be active and have no time for themselves, progress is very slow or even non-existent.

Having been brought up to believe that doing nothing is wrong and wasteful, while doing something is productive and good, people often find it difficult to change their ways. In my opinion, doing nothing can be doing something very important.

Case History

Joe was stressed and came to see me for advice. He was working a 60-hour week, and when he returned home the needs of his wife and two young children occupied him till bedtime. I explained the importance of quiet time and taught him a relaxation procedure to practise daily.

He returned two weeks later, apologising for the fact that he had not done any relaxation. 'My wife won't let me lie down for 20 minutes doing nothing. She says it's a waste of time when there are so many things to do around the house.'

We discussed the attitude of his wife and I asked, 'Do you think she would allow you to listen to a relaxation tape?'

Joe thought that might be acceptable, so I gave him a tape, and when he returned for the next session he said he was feeling a lot better, less stressed with more energy. 'My wife thinks it's a very good idea to listen to the tape because at least I'm doing something worthwhile!'

The techniques involved in relaxation, meditation or self-hypnosis all enhance the benefits of quiet time. The fact that you are giving yourself some time is also relevant to the benefit achieved.

The alpha state can be achieved simply by meditating in a chair, but many people achieve it by physical exercise or listening to quiet music. Repetitive active movements, such as those involved in jogging, swimming or walking, can lull us into a relaxed state and clear the mind of clutter. Patients frequently tell me how much better they feel after swimming 20 lengths of the pool or jogging for half an hour. The means is less important than the end.

It is important to remember that you will not *find* time for yourself – you need to *make* it. Acknowledging this distinction indicates the seriousness of your intention. Too many people tell themselves that they will find the time, but they never do; that phraseology shows less commitment than 'I will make the time'.

Many people find it best to set aside 20 minutes at a similar time each day so that a routine develops. Find a time and place where you will not be disturbed or have to dash off immediately afterwards. For some this can be in the morning before work; for others it can be after returning from work, perhaps in the bath. The only unsuitable time is in bed at night, as you might drift off to sleep (delta rhythm) rather than staying in alpha rhythm.

How to Meditate

- Ensure you have 20 uninterrupted minutes to yourself, which are not followed immediately by some pressing engagement.
- Find a safe, comfortable place where you can lie or sit with your head supported. If you are too comfortable, you might go to sleep.
- Close your eyes and focus on your breathing. Allow the regularity of the breathing to help you relax. Tell yourself that there is nothing to do, nothing else matters. Just be there and be aware that you are giving yourself a present of time.
- Allow thoughts to drift in and out of your mind, don't try to stop them: they are just thoughts, and as you are not in a position to deal with them for a little while, simply let them go.
- Allow yourself to relax by accepting whatever thoughts or feelings you have. Develop a floating, drifting feeling, perhaps by imagining how it feels to be a leaf floating down from a tree.
- Just *be* there, focus on your exhalations and allow the rhythm to relax you. Become an impartial observer of your thoughts as they drift by.
- Be aware of any bodily sensations, but don't try to alter them as they indicate what level of relaxation you are achieving.

- Remain involved in this process for 20 minutes, but tell yourself that time is of no significance. If you like, you can set an alarm clock before you start, but generally the mind has a very accurate clock of its own.
- When you feel ready to return to the room, focus on your inhalations, allowing yourself to come back to the waking state in your own way and your own time.
- Open your eyes, have a stretch and take a little while before reverting to the beta state of trying.

Quiet time is a simple concept, perhaps so simple that people are unaware of its benefits and do not make use of it. Be aware that quiet time provides an antidote to everyday pressures, allowing emotions to be more harmonious with attitudes, thoughts and behaviour.

20

Asking the Right Questions

'If we can really understand the problem, the answer will come out
of it because the answer is not separate from the problem.'

KRISHNAMURTI

Learning is most commonly achieved by asking questions, so
this chapter examines the questioning process and suggests ways
of improving the questions we ask to get the most helpful
answers.

If you are flying to a holiday destination and ask the question, 'What if the plane crashes?' you will respond very differently
than to the question, 'How long will it take to get a good tan on
the beach?'

There are many different ways of asking questions.

In medical training most questions are directed towards what
is wrong, what illness or pathology is present. These questions
lead to a cause, and thus help to find a solution. Medical students
study illness not health; they ask 'Why is he ill?' rather than 'Why
is he healthy?'

In physical medicine the question 'How did he break his leg?'
is less important than 'What can we do to fix it?' Sometimes this
approach is successful too in psychological medicine. In many
instances clients can be helped without knowing the basic cause
of their problems.

Our thought processes are turned in whichever direction the
question leads us. If we ask, 'Why?' we seek an answer through
analysis; if we ask, 'What was the cause?' we search in the past

for an answer; if we ask, 'What would we like to happen?' we are focusing on positive options for the future.

In order to resolve problems, the questions we ask ourselves need to be tailored to guide us through a maze of options towards a solution. It is no use ruminating over a question that has been asked again and again: the only consequence will be to add despair to the original problem. As in a maze, if we repeatedly arrive at the same point, frustration and anger diminish our endeavours.

In psychological medicine there are many avenues leading clients towards health. Some focus on the past in order to gain insight and understanding; others utilise behaviour to learn new ways of acting; still others teach us to alter restrictive beliefs and avoid false conclusions. Whatever the approach, the universal aim is to tailor therapy to the client's needs.

Brief Therapy

As its name suggests, brief therapy is tailored to those whose time and income are limited. The questions it asks are more likely to be 'How?' 'What?' or 'When?' than 'Why?' For example, 'How do you feel now about last week's experience?' or 'What would happen if you acted this way instead?' or 'When do you think it would be suitable to make the change we are discussing?'

All these questions guide the client towards the present or future: the past is accepted as having passed and not being relevant to the future. Minimal emphasis is placed on childhood experiences, as these are deemed unchangeable: spending time analysing them is thought unnecessary for improvement. Tasks are set and new strategies employed to encourage changes in attitudes, beliefs and behaviour. The aim of such tactics is to help clients get off the roundabout that is taking them in circles and preventing progress.

Solution-focused therapy

This is a brief therapy that directs clients towards their strengths and abilities. Specific questions create awareness of positive attitudes and experiences, which are lost when focusing on problems rather than solutions. Treatment is aimed at reinforcing successful behaviour instead of dwelling on deficiencies – the carrot rather than the stick. Discussions continually guide the client away from the problem and towards the solution.

I call this approach 'panning for gold' because the client/miner knows his pan is full of mud: his aim is to seek out the specks of gold that will make him rich.

Solution-focused therapy uses language that guides the client towards the 'specks of gold', increasing optimism, energy and expectation.

> **Client:** 'Doctor, my relationship with my husband is so bad that we argue all the time.'
> **Therapist:** 'Are there any times in the day that you don't argue?'
> **Client:** 'Well, yes, I suppose there must be. We occasionally talk civilly to each other at mealtimes.'
> **Therapist:** 'Tell me about these times. What happens when they occur, how do you feel, and in what way do you communicate when you are "talking civilly"?'

The client complains about the bad times ('We argue all the time'), so the therapist endeavours to alter the client's perspective to notice when things are better and what she is doing to cause this. In this way the client learns to do more of what works rather than focusing on what doesn't work. Being aware when things are going well enables us to create similar situations again and again.

In his book *Healing the Whole Person* Dr Robert McNeilly gives many examples of how certain questions have promoted rapid and lasting improvements in emotions and behaviour. By constantly focusing on positive outcomes and enabling clients to become aware of their strengths he helps them to realise first that they can change and second that they already possess the tools to do so. In all cases, the therapist's task is to be skilful enough to help the client realise these two facts.

A case history from Dr McNeilly's book illustrates how questions can help clients discover their own resources.

A 40-year-old woman sought help for difficulties at work. She sold insurance over the phone and trained sales people to deal with difficult customers. She was troubled by her new boss who was rude, demanding and unsupportive. During the first session Dr McNeilly asked her, 'Is your new boss a difficult customer?' She thought long and hard about this reframe, then a smile crept across her face. 'Thank you,' she said, 'I'll be all right now.' And she was. The question had helped her to make a connection between the 'problem boss' and her own resources, enabling her to realise she had the capability and techniques to deal with him.

Living with Catastrophe

Some unfortunate people are forced to live with what I call a 'catastrophiser' in their minds. This parasite causes untold damage simply by using the two words 'What if . . .' followed by a scene of doom and gloom. The results of such behaviour are fear and avoidance, especially if there are past experiences to support the catastrophiser. For example, the notion 'I think I'll fly to America this summer' is quickly followed by the catastrophiser saying 'What if the plane crashes? Who will look after my wife and children?'

This destructive internal voice is an unwanted tenant in the mind, casting doubt in areas that are unpredictable because they are all in the future. It is on safe ground as we cannot say with certainty that it is wrong. The 'What if?' question creates fear, uncertainty and worry. It points us in the direction of danger so that we can use avoidance to maintain some semblance of control.

Although the catastrophiser usually worries about the future, it sometimes directs its attention to the past: 'What if it happens again?'

The response to this question dredges up undesirable emotions relating to previous experiences, engulfing the client with an instant replay and causing concern about the future. The question acts as a bridge, linking past problems to future doubts. In theory, this question is a protective device; in practice, it causes the problem it is trying to prevent.

The 'What if?' question creates a state of alertness similar to that of a sprinter waiting for the starter's gun to fire and it never does. Adrenaline courses through his body, anticipation puts him on edge, energy drains away and the prolonged state of heightened tension causes anxiety and exhaustion.

In everyday life such an attitude can have many physical and psychological effects, including burnout, panic attacks, phobias and numerous other symptoms of stress.

Overcoming Catastrophe

How do we deal with a catastrophiser living in our mind? It is not easy, as the unwanted tenant has generally been in residence for years and was placed there by brainwashing received in childhood.

First, we need to be aware of its existence, notice the repeated 'What ifs?' that are circulating in our mind. We need to realise that they are only words, that they come from within ourselves, and that we must break the connection between the words and the emotional response that follows. Just as a victim must learn how to deal with a bully, so we must learn how to deal with the catastrophiser.

Once you become aware of the 'What ifs?' there are a number of responses you can choose.

1. **Ignore the question.** This is difficult but possible. By recognising it as merely words created by past experiences and not relevant to the present, we can learn to ignore it and

hear it as a sound. Just as in a restaurant we hear people at the next table but are able to ignore what they say, so we can tune out the catastrophiser.

By ignoring the question we break the feedback loop (see chapter 8) that is reinforcing the catastrophiser. The more we take notice of the question, the more insistent it becomes. The more we regard it as just a nuisance, the more likely it is to go away.

2. **Respond with a positive scenario.** Look at the following example:

> **You:** 'I'm giving a presentation next week.'
> **Catastrophiser:** 'What if you dry up and can't speak?'
> **You:** 'What if I give the best speech of my life?'

The 'What ifs?' are about the future, so there is no certainty about what will happen. The catastrophiser cannot deny the positive response even if it brings past experiences to support its claim.

3. **Learn who the catastrophiser is representing.** Generally, it is someone of influence from the past who has been 'ingested' and now resides in your mind. Challenge this character, talk to it, learn about its personality and aims. Inform it that it resides in your head as a tenant, and unless it behaves, you will evict it, just as you would any unwanted tenant in real life.

Visualise this character (see chapter 24) and spend quiet time coming to terms with it. Imagine you are a powerful landlord with right on your side: be assertive and don't get caught up with any theoretical discussions about what might happen. Catastrophisers are generally very wily and have all the answers. Say 'no' repeatedly in a firm, confident voice to the 'What ifs'.

Questions of Emotion

Questions often lead to emotions, either questions we ask ourselves or those asked by others. There are many factors involved in producing these emotions – who asks the question, the tone of voice, the content of the question, and the situation in which it occurs.

Questions *about* emotions can also bring awareness, allowing expression and resolution. For example:

'What am I feeling?'
'What is happening (inside or outside) to cause this feeling?'
'Is this feeling helpful (appropriate, suitable)?'
'What was the trigger that caused this feeling?'

All these questions help us learn more about our feelings, and as understanding is a major factor in resolution, the more we are aware of what is happening, the easier it will be to deal with. Questions are like scraps of paper in a paper chase – their function is to lead us to our intended goal. Each question has the capacity to help us appreciate a number of things – our abilities, the times when we succeeded, the feelings in our emotional pool and the goals we wish to achieve. Unsuitable questions lead us astray or around in circles.

Questions of Criticism

Another question that leads us into a brick wall of negative emotion is, 'What will people think?'

This is both very common and very limiting. It creates anxiety, guilt and shame, and creates an avoidance philosophy. People who continually ask this question are playing a dangerous game called 'mind reading'. It is dangerous because it is impossible to find the answer and raises negative conjectures. How *could* we know what people think? If we ask them, they are unlikely to give us an honest reply, and who are these people anyway?

Answering the question 'What will people think?' is part of a psychological process called projection, in which we attribute our own thoughts to others.

Case History

Clare had a good job as personal assistant to the manager of a software company. She was doing well with her job, receiving bonuses and praise, but was concerned about one specific area. She was not highly educated and was constantly worried in case someone realised this and she lost her job.

Everyone at work was happy with Clare's performance, but she repeatedly asked me during our consultation, 'What will people think if they find out I have only two O levels?' The question haunted her, making her feel anxious and lose sleep.

During our consultation Clare learnt that she was projecting her own concerns onto others. I told her, 'The real question is what do *you* think about your lack of education?' This question formed the basis of the next two consultations and helped her to realise that it was possible to feel good about herself, her ability and her work in spite of her limited qualifications. As her confidence grew, she was able to discuss her concern with a close friend at work. This discussion relieved her and made her feel less under the spotlight. She focused more on the present, her own thoughts about herself and on what she was actually doing until the question 'What will people think?' faded from her vocabulary.

Questions of the Future

A very useful question that directs our attention to positive events in the future is: 'Won't it be wonderful when . . . ?'

The response to this question in the mind/body complex is a favourable one, producing optimistic thoughts and feelings. It triggers the creative part of the mind to form pictures of the situation you hope to achieve. It oils the machinery of the mind, making a positive future more accessible and providing hope and energy to achieve it.

'Won't it be wonderful when ... ?' distracts us away from past ruminations or present concerns, allowing us to spend time imagining and creating what we hope for. Time spent this way encourages us to create a framework necessary to achieve our aims.

Questions of Assumption

Another form of question has the goal implied as an assumed fact. For example, a mother wanting her child to have a bath might say, 'Would you like to have a bath before or after you watch television?' This focuses attention on the timing rather than the bathing.

A similar strategy is used on public signs, such as 'Thank you for not smoking', which implies that you are not smoking so it doesn't need to request you not to.

You Have the Answer

People seeking therapy are seeking change. Sometimes, however, they become so involved in this quest that they lose sight of the complete picture and are only aware of the problem that needs changing. Constructing suitable questions enables us to take a fresh look at problems, gain new insight and see a more balanced picture.

For example, asking 'What in your life does not need changing?' gives us an opportunity to reflect on things that are going well but are often ignored, overshadowed or taken for granted. The right question helps us to realise that the problem is only a small part of our lives and that we are not so hopeless and helpless as we believe.

21

Expressing Emotions

'When we can talk about worries they cease to have power over us.'
JEANNETTE WINTERSON, WRITER

If questioning our internal processes leads to greater under-standing of our emotions, it follows that learning how to express them must also be beneficial. This chapter looks at ways in which this can be achieved.

Emotions can be regarded as fluid energy within the mind/body system – stored, circulated and released in specific situations. They are a natural phenomenon, designed to aid survival, but if confined, may build up and cause problems.

Emotions cause an arousal state compared to the dampening effect of rest, relaxation or sleep. Arousal means activity, or readi-ness for activity, created by nervous, muscular or hormonal factors. As previously mentioned the word emotion is derived from the Latin: 'to move, excite, stir up or agitate'; and so it aptly represents the arousal situation.

Emotion is like a river flowing down the mountains to the sea. It is fed by various components, joins up with numerous tributaries, and sometimes suffers from excess. Should any blockage occur, pressure builds and the banks burst, flooding the surrounding area. Removal of the blockage allows the over-flow to subside and drain away.

Experiences produce feelings painful or pleasant, depending on the situation. If the emotion is painful, it may be suppressed, like a dam holds back water, to prevent its release. It requires energy to prevent these suppressed, unresolved emotions (see chapter 11) escaping to the conscious mind, but they are still present and active beyond our awareness.

Another way in which unpleasant emotions are kept at bay is a process called repression, which means to put down. The emotions are put down in the unconscious to keep them from harming us consciously. This mechanism operates on an unconscious level to protect us from ideas, impulses or memories that cause anxiety, apprehension or guilt. Both the emotion and the process repressing the emotion are out of our control as they reside in the unconscious mind. When repressed memories are triggered (see chapter 10), they break out of unconscious captivity and flood the mind/body system.

Case History

Robin had many self-imposed restrictions (dams) blocking his emotional flow. He grew up in a regimented household where his father, being a military man, insisted that army rules be applied. As a child, strict discipline was the order of the day, and any transgressions were regarded as failures. Robin learnt rules about right and wrong, good and bad, success and failure that bore no resemblance to society's norms. He was bullied at school because he was 'weak'; he wasn't top of his class because he was a 'failure'; when he expressed emotions he was a 'sissy'. His internal landscape was shaped by restrictive rules, and his father would not tolerate any discussion on the matter.

In his twenties Robin sought an army career and was very successful, but he came to see me for help with public speaking. An expression of shame came over his face as he described his 'weakness' and 'failure' some years previously when he dried up while giving a talk to his fellow officers.

It had since been a terrifying ordeal to stand on a podium and talk because memories of his 'failure' haunted him, causing panic and fear in case his 'weakness' would occur again.

The dam that Robin had built prevented the flow of any

emotion that allowed him to view his situation in a non-judgemental way. His father's critical words coloured all his perceptions.

The work Robin and I did was focused on removing the dam, allowing him to express his feelings without labelling them negatively as his father had done. This allowed him to realise that he was like everyone else – comfortable in most areas of his life but uncomfortable in a few. He was eventually able to comment to his audience that he was nervous giving the lecture, something he never would have dreamed of doing before. He was then pleasantly surprised by some who confessed that they felt the same way too.

As Robin grew to understand his suppression mechanism, take risks and learn from mistakes, so the words failure and weakness occurred less and less in his vocabulary.

Emotional Ways and Means

Emotions may be regarded as having a three-stage cycle in the mind/body system: stimulus, build-up and release. This cycle maintains an internal balance. If blocked, the emotional energy seeks alternative outlets, causing symptoms and distress. The points below look at some of the ways in which emotional energy is diverted, preventing us from exploring and expressing our feelings.

- As survival is our prime goal, the most important process of the mind/body system is a mechanism to create safety. Anything that threatens survival, such as abandonment, will trigger this emergency process, just as a burglar entering a home will trigger the burglar alarm.
- If, in childhood, we express emotions and are made to feel frightened, guilty, ridiculed or shamed, we learn to suppress rather than express emotions for safety reasons.

- Repeated unpleasant situations can lead to repeated suppressions, resulting in the belief: 'I stopped the feeling and survived, so I must continue to do this as I know it works.' This suppression of feelings becomes a reflex response associated with internal messages, such as 'Feelings are dangerous – they cause trouble, confusion, punishment'. The conclusion is therefore, 'It is safer to suppress feelings than release them'.

- Some children in Bosnia were asked to draw aspects of the war that had affected them. One nine-year-old boy drew his house being bombed by aeroplanes. Underneath his picture he wrote, 'I must be a very naughty boy because they are bombing our house.' When, as children, we become involved in a situation we fear but do not understand, we seek a release to make it less uncomfortable. By resorting to self-blame, 'It was my fault', we feel a little better as we have found a solution (albeit incorrect) to the puzzle. The tension is reduced and we develop a habit of self-blame which, over a period of time, feels normal.

- The body and mind have different approaches to unpleasant feelings. The body pushes to release them, while the mind has learnt ways to keep them battened down. Energy is required in the conflict between these two desires.

- Over time it is possible to become so used to tension that we develop a feeling of comfort in our discomfort. Any release from the discomfort causes concern, confusion and fear, as we feel out of control, so we return to the former mode of behaviour even if it is causing problems.

- When we learn that it is safe to express feelings, the body and mind work together, the head finding the language to translate the physical sensations felt by the body.

- One mechanism that repeats itself throughout life is separation anxiety. It occurs at birth when we are separated from the womb, and may continue in one form or another thereafter. This anxiety causes concern about change, so many people bypass it by avoiding change and using all their energy to maintain the status quo.

- A build-up of emotions over time causes many people to be concerned about releasing them. For example: 'I've been angry at my mother for years. If I start to tell her about my feelings, it will get out of hand and I'll regret it. The situation as it is means I'm in control: once I start to let go, I don't know where it will end. I'm sure I'll open a can of worms if I confront her.' This is an avoidance mechanism that becomes a block.

- Babies have emotions too, but as they lack the speech to communicate verbally, they use other methods. These pre-verbal emotions are stored in their original state, and as adults we cannot contact them on an intellectual level as there are no words for expression. Techniques such as primal scream, re-birthing, psychodrama, hypnosis and regression therapy are some of the ways these emotions can be accessed and expressed.

- The conditions necessary for expressing emotions are trust, safety, support, care and security: when these are present, emotions flow easily; when they are absent, the process is blocked.

- Emotions are often described as good or bad, positive or negative, right or wrong. It would be preferable to categorise them as suitable or unsuitable, appropriate or inappropriate, helpful or unhelpful, accurate or misleading.

- A build-up of emotional tension can be indicated by physical or mental symptoms. The body or mind is letting us know that there is excess energy in the emotional systems. We then have the conscious choice of taking notice of these symptom messages and releasing excess emotional energy, or blocking them and creating problems.

- Emotions are often more clearly expressed by actions than words. Blushing, perspiring or fidgeting, for example, betray how we feel without any conscious volition: emotion simply trickles or floods its way to expression.

- The main benefit of expressing emotions is that it achieves release which in turn creates *relief*. This is a balanced, calm, state enabling us to focus on daily activities without distraction.

- As a general rule, emotions can be regarded as messages from the body to the mind. Our aim is to decipher these emotional messages and check if they are suitable and appropriate for our needs. If they are out of date or inappropriate messages, we need to improve them so that they become helpful and accurate.

How to Express Emotions

The aim of expressing emotions is to release them from your mind/body complex. This does not mean that you need a response from someone else. In fact, it is often preferable if the expression is not related to an anticipated response, as generally we do not get the response we wish for. Letting the feeling out of your system is the first step in the release–relief pathway.

- If you can tell someone how you feel at the time the emotion is occurring, it will prevent an incubation of the emotion. Sometimes this is not possible because we realise what we would like to say after the experience has passed. In these cases it is suitable to talk about it later.
- 'When you said you thought Tom was a cheat, I felt very hurt as he is one of my best friends.' This comment is made without anger or blame: you are simply sharing your emotion. In this way it is released from your body and you can deal with whatever response occurs. It is much less confrontational than 'You were very mean to say that my friend Tom was a cheat.' Remember your aim is to be heard, not to offer blame or criticism or to dump your angry feelings on someone else. Choose your time carefully for such comments as the other person must be in the right frame of mind to receive them.
- If it is not possible to vocalise your emotions because you

are too nervous or the other person is unavailable, try writing down your feelings in a letter, expressing them as graphically as you can, then burn the letter to release the imprisoned emotions. The 'ceremonial' burning adds weight to the experience, which can be repeated every time the emotions build up.

- Sharing feelings with a friend diminishes their intensity. The aim is to release the feelings, not to get a suitable response from your friend. In order to achieve this, you need a supportive, attentive listener, not one offering judgement, advice or solutions. If you believe it is too much for a friend to cope with, it might be better to seek professional help from a counsellor.

- Activities are often very successful outlets for emotions. Whether active, like sport and gardening, or cerebral, like painting and stamp collecting, activities combine pleasure with distraction (see chapter 9).

- There are various techniques specifically designed for emotional release, including re-birthing, psychodrama, primal scream therapy, autogenic training, hypnotherapy and body work. You can explore the possibilities of these techniques with a professional counsellor.

While expressing emotion can be difficult after years of blockage, once the process is started, it's like a syphon that tends to flow by itself. Inappropriate and out-of-date emotions stored for years can only cause harm. Releasing them allows space to be yourself in the present without being weighed down by events from the past.

22
Manual Therapy

'The body never lies.'

MARTHA GRAHAM, AMERICAN DANCER

Articulating emotions is perhaps the most usual way of releasing them, but physical techniques can provide equally effective means of release. This chapter examines a variety of physical treatments and shows how they can be directly related to emotional responses.

William is a quiet, sensitive osteopath who has a busy practice in Manchester, and we meet from time to time to discuss the different perspectives we have about therapy. He uses his strong hands as well as his listening skills to help clients suffering from a variety of conditions. We both agree that the mind and body are interwoven in the symptoms presented to us. He calls his technique 'manual therapy' because of his hands-on approach.

During one of our discussions, William mentioned that he often released emotions by using solar plexus pressure. The solar plexus is a highly sensitive network of nerves and ganglia situated behind the stomach, which radiates like the sun (hence 'solar') to supply all the abdominal organs. It is connected to the brain by a major nerve called the vagus, and has long been held as a symbolic centre of emotion (see chapter 5).

I was very interested in William's comments as I knew of the body's ability to store emotions but had never been involved in their release by physical pressure. I asked him to tell me more about his manual therapy.

'If I notice clients holding themselves stiffly or breathing in an awkward manner, I like to explore the part that is tight or rigid. Sometimes it is their breathing that gives them away: instead of breathing smoothly from the diaphragm, they breathe with their chest, or erratically in jerky movements, and I know they are holding their abdominal muscles tight and tense. When I notice this erratic breathing I ask the client to lie down and gently feel the tension in the abdominal muscles. If I meet a firmness, I start to exert gentle pressure over the solar plexus area, as I know emotions will be stored there. The muscle tension is a response to the holding in of unresolved feelings.

'Traumatic experiences create strong emotions that are either dealt with and resolved, or repressed and hidden in the mind or body. Repressed emotions, like a log-jam on a river, cause problems. If the obstruction can be cleared and the logs freed, the river will flow smoothly and carry its cargo to a suitable destination.

'So it is with emotions. They flow around the body and mind every day, and when one becomes stuck (not resolved) the whole system becomes jammed and problems arise. It may take some time for the problems to surface as symptoms, but they always do, and in order to return the client to health, we need to deal with the role of either the mind or the body in maintaining the problem. Solar plexus pressure concentrates on the body.

'I only proceed if it feels right for me to do so, and the client accepts what I am trying to do. Sometimes the muscles are so tense that I realise whatever emotions are hidden beneath them they will not respond to my therapy, so I refer the client to a psychotherapist. At other times, nothing happens during the session, but memories surface in the days that follow. I can generally feel the muscles relax layer by layer, and it is the most tense muscle layers that seem to protect the really traumatic memories. Just as hypnosis delves into the deeper levels of the mind, so solar plexus pressure probes into deeper muscle levels, the depth generally representing the time when the trauma occurred. If it was in childhood, I may need to dig really deeply.'

William's experience was that pressure on the muscles alters a feedback loop (see chapter 6) between the brain and the solar plexus. Traumatic memories stored in the brain send nervous messages to the solar plexus, causing tension in the abdominal organs and muscles, which then send nervous impulses back to the brain to complete the loop. The hidden emotion – muscle tension loop can be broken either by dealing with the stored emotion using psychotherapy, or altering the muscle pressure with manual therapy. In either case, the emotion comes to consciousness and can be resolved, allowing a healthy feedback loop to be re-established.

Case History

William told me about a 26-year-old client of his called Anna. She had suffered from muscle tension and back pain for a long time but had no idea what was causing it. Visits to chiropractors and other therapists had yielded no benefit. When William examined Anna he found many of her muscles in spasm, especially those radiating from the back to the neck. After listening to her and asking pertinent questions, he discussed solar plexus pressure with her and she agreed to let him proceed.

As William pressed on Anna's abdominal muscles, he sensed something stored underneath. He continued the pressure for about four minutes and suddenly Anna burst into uncontrollable sobbing. She continued crying in a hysterical way for many minutes, unable to speak or explain what was happening. He remained with her in a passive, comforting role, allowing her emotions to well up. As Anna was his last patient for the day, he was able to stay with her for the two hours she needed to settle down. During those hours she was able to relate between tears what had surfaced following his abdominal pressure.

'I was suddenly overcome by a terrible feeling of fear and helplessness,' she said. 'I could see the face of this friend of mine, a man I knew years ago. He was bending over me and I could feel the weight of his body on me. I realised he was raping me and it all came back so vividly I can remember every detail.

'It happened five years ago when we went out on a date. I felt funny after dinner but I didn't remember anything more about that night until you were pushing on my muscles, then it suddenly came into my mind, like a horror movie. I think he must have put something in my drink. It's so amazing that I could have blocked off such a horrible experience for so long. Why did it come back now?'

William spent time explaining what he believed had happened to release this deeply hidden incident. He saw Anna for the next few weeks to help her talk about her experience and the associated emotions, and gradually she began to feel better and the muscles all over her body relaxed.

How can we explain Anna's story and William's technique?

If we regard the mind/body system as an entity with inter-connecting nervous and chemical systems sending messages back and forth, we can understand how activity in one creates a response in the other.

We could postulate that there is a threshold in the system, above which a protective mechanism comes into play. In Anna's case, the horror of the rape was above her threshold, so her mind used its protective mechanism to repress the experience (perhaps aided by the drug used by the rapist), and the muscles went into spasm as a result of the trauma. It is interesting to note that the muscle spasms and pain were increasing with time rather than decreasing as one would expect if a healing process were taking place. When conditions do not resolve with time, one should be aware that there are factors at work preventing natural resolu-tion. In such cases interventions like William's are necessary to aid the body's ability to heal.

William's treatment highlights the vast network of nervous and chemical transmissions that reside in the body, which carry messages that cause physical or emotional changes. If we see something frightening, for example, we immediately tense up, our heart races and our hands perspire. The nervous system is carrying the image we saw and transforming it into bodily changes. It follows that if we change our posture, we can alter how we feel. Strictures such as 'Keep your chin up' and 'shoulders back' indicate the connection between posture and emotions.

The main thing I learn from my discussions with William is that there are many ways to approach clients' problems. The direct approach to tense muscles can sometimes cause an instantaneous response. Analytic therapy, on the other hand, builds a picture like a jigsaw, while hypnosis delves into different levels of the unconscious. The art of the therapist is to know which therapy is going to be most suitable for which client.

23

From Pain to Pleasure –
Reframing and Distraction

'As you go through life, make this your goal. Keep your
eye upon the doughnut and not upon the hole.'

This chapter examines two techniques that can help us to maintain emotional equilibrium. The first is reframing, which helps
us to take a different perspective on life. The second is distraction, which helps take our mind off things.

The basis of both reframing and distraction is that feelings
are related to attitudes, not to specific events. In other words,
it's not what we look at but how we look at it that determines
our feelings.

Reframing

This technique involves changing the mind-set – a thought
process that determines our view of things – to see things differently. A racist, for example, may have a mind-set that views black
people as inferior to whites; a liberal person would regard them
as equal. Black people are what they are, but those two views
create completely different attitudes.

A client of mine recalled an unkind form of reframing during
her childhood: 'When I was young I waited for the ice-cream

man to come to our area, but when I told Mum he was ringing his bell, she said, "He does that to let you know he has run out of ice-cream," so I never had any.'

The mother had reframed the situation so that she would not have to buy ice-cream for her daughter.

Steps to reframing

1. Have an open and flexible mind-set. If the mind-set is rigid and fixed, it is not possible to alter your perspective. If, for example, you declare that 'Everyone knows the glass is half empty and that's that,' you are not open to seeing it as half-full.

2. Create a desire for change. Motivation is always a major factor in making any personal improvement. It is very difficult to change if the energy is not present, or if someone else's energy is desiring the change. For example, 'I'm coming to see you to stop smoking because my wife says it's a filthy habit.'

   'Do you want to stop?'

   'Not really. I enjoy it and don't think I'll be able to change.'

3. Become aware of what you are telling yourself that is creating the negative feeling. Examine your belief system and the comparisons you are making. Changing these things will lead to an improvement in mood.

   A woman had an obsession with cleaning the house. She hoovered constantly and admonished her husband and sons for their untidiness. Eventually, she realised her attitude was obsessive and sought help from a therapist.

   The therapist said to her, 'Imagine a lovely new fluffy carpet, no footprints on it and you are sitting in the centre.'

   'That feels wonderful,' the woman replied.

   'Now realise that means you are completely isolated from your husband and sons – they cannot get close to you.'

   The woman burst into tears and immediately changed her behaviour towards cleaning. Whereas she had regarded it as essential and wonderful, the therapist reframed the activity to show it as isolating and lonely.

Changing the words we use to describe our attitude can help to reframe a situation and make it more manageable. For example, referring to something as a nuisance rather than a problem immediately lessens its importance. This view makes the situation easier to live with and can free us of the need to fix things. We become acceptors, saving time and energy in the process. This strategy is described in more detail in chapter 16.

4. Use lateral thinking to create a reframe. This method has been popularised by psychologist Edward de Bono, who has written many books on the subject. The normal, linear way of thinking moves from step A to B to C, etc., while lateral thinking has an alternative viewpoint that may not follow a logical progression.

For example, a city council found an ingenious solution to the problem of cars parking for a long time in its over-subscribed car parks. At the entrance to the car parks it placed large signs that read: 'Cars may be parked here as long as you like. The only requirement is that headlights must be left on. Any car without headlights on will be fined.'

Lateral thinking involves using the creative right hemi-sphere of the brain rather than the logical left hemisphere. The best way to tap into this is by relaxing and allowing random thoughts, however ridiculous, to enter your mind. You may be surprised when you suddenly think of an ingenious solution.

5. Repeat 'It really doesn't matter' in your mind like a mantra to relieve the pressure of whatever is worrying you. Although these words might seem simplistic, they are actu-ally true – most worries really don't matter in the grand scheme of things. Using 'It really doesn't matter' as a base-line reduces concerns to a manageable scale and prevents negative emotions from draining your energy. Think of the neighbours from hell fighting over a few inches of land

and ending up in court paying thousands of pounds in legal fees: if they had the attitude 'It really doesn't matter', a lot of time, emotion and expense would be saved.

6. Find something positive about the concern you have. This will often show the way out of an apparently intractable situation.

Years ago a young doctor was put in charge of a psychiatric ward with severely disturbed patients. One of these patients was a 40-year-old man with catatonic schizophrenia, a condition that makes the arms and legs rigid. The man had not been outside the ward for many years.

The doctor asked himself, 'What is good about this man's condition and how can I help him by making use of this?' He thought long and hard, then visited an art class in the neighbouring town. 'Would you like a superb model who will sit still for hours?' he asked. The offer was accepted, so the man was driven to the art class daily and became their most illustrious model. After some months there was a marked improvement in his condition.

7. Seek other information that may improve the perspective.

Some years ago, when I lived in Melbourne, I was travelling in a very crowded tram when the person behind me stood on my heel causing severe pain. We were packed in like sardines, so it was difficult to turn around. When it happened again I became very angry, saying to myself, 'If he does that again, I'll turn around and tell him what I think of him.'

Some minutes later it happened again and I turned around, ready to abuse the person who had stood on my heel three times. As I did so, I saw he was a man with a white stick and my anger disappeared in a flash.

There is a lovely book called *The Sensuous Garden* by Monty Don (see Further Reading), in which he writes about the garden from a sensuous point of view: the rustle of leaves, the fragrance of flowers, the textures of plants, the taste of produce, and the sights that change daily. He gives a new perspective on the garden, urging us to ignore the instructional approach of many books and experts, and to enjoy the garden in our own personal way and appreciating whatever takes our fancy. It's a delightful way of reframing how we approach nature.

Distraction

Possibly the most common pathway from pain to pleasure is via distraction, and we learn it at an early age. The child who refuses to eat, for example, is encouraged to have 'One spoonful for Granny and one spoonful for Grandpa . . .' The attention is diverted from the food by the thought of doing something for someone else. Distraction directs us away from the upset towards something more pleasant. We continue to use this technique throughout life: listening to music, for example, changes our mood, while seeing a funny film helps us to forget problems.

Many people believe they have to be constantly distracted by activities in order to keep their depression at bay: 'I never relax because I'm frightened how I might feel. It's as if I'm letting go, losing control, and from past experience I fear I will plummet into a black mood.'

This unbalanced approach to activity/relaxation is when problems occur. Energy is drained by excess activity. Quiet time is an important ingredient for a balanced life, but when I ask clients to sit quietly for half an hour a day, the look of horror on their faces tells me it will not happen.

We can create helpful distractions in all kinds of situations: I count the steps I take if I am carrying something heavy to distract me from the discomfort of the weight, while thoughts of happier times can decrease feelings of fear, anger, guilt and sadness. Other distractions, such as comfort eating, alcohol and tobacco, may also serve the purpose, but their health implications mean that they cannot really be considered helpful.

It is impossible to have negative feelings if we are entirely focused on a pleasurable pastime, hence the benefit of exercise and sport. Many people tell me how wonderful they feel after going to the gym – the combination of exercise and distraction changes their mood completely. Similarly, the company of good friends can divert attention away from the thoughts and feelings that upset or depress us.

Hobbies also play a major role in altering how we feel. Whether you indulge in stamp collecting or wood-turning, the important thing is the passion: when it absorbs us completely, there is no room for negative emotions.

Finding a technique to distract yourself when necessary is an artform that aids life. Unlike avoidance, which is a head-in-the sand approach, distraction is a conscious short-term pleasure that can make us better able to cope in the long term.

24
Helpful Techniques to Improve Emotions

'If you give a man a fish, you feed him for a day.
If you teach him how to fish, you feed him for life.'
PROVERB

There are a number of techniques I use to help people overcome problems with emotion. All of them involve learning about yourself, so they require quiet time and dedication to be effective. The aim is to understand the process in the mind/body system that is causing problems, and to alter this process so that resolution occurs.

The Affect Bridge

'Affect' is another word for 'emotion', and the principle of this technique is to connect or bridge feelings in the present with those stored in the emotional pool relating to past experience. The connection is made by using feelings that occur in the intervening years as stepping stones. The theory behind this simple exercise is as follows:

- We have an experience in the past that causes an unwanted emotion that is not resolved.

- This emotion is continually being triggered by present-day events.
- By focusing on the feeling and counting back through time, we can arrive at the original source.
- We can then become more aware of the original cause and release it by discussion, recognition and writing, and in this way remove it as a target for future triggers.

How to use the affect bridge technique

1. Arrange for yourself to have quiet time when you will not be disturbed.
2. Focus on the feeling to be explored – note where it is in your body and feel it. Go into the part of your body where the feeling resides and use it as a barometer to judge the intensity of feeling in subsequent steps.
3. Slowly count back from your present age, noting the years when the feeling increases in intensity.
4. When you have counted back to nought, think about the years when the feeling increased. Note what emotional experiences may have been relevant during those times.
5. Write down each of the experiences and how you felt at the time.
6. View those experiences and associated emotions from the present time: talk to yourself about them and allow rationality to enter the discussion. Put these emotions and experiences into the perspective of an adult person: note changes and improvements that have occurred in your life since then.
7. At a later date, talk about the feelings: release them by sharing your experiences with someone you can trust.
8. Think how you would like to integrate these experiences into your life now. Allow the passage of time to dilute the feelings and help them to be more up to date and appropriate. Repeat this exercise daily for one week so that the process of resolution can really occur.

Case History

Lucy was an anxious woman of 50. She was married with two children, and, in her own words, was a 'born worrier'. Her problem was anxiety attacks in the supermarket. She could go when accompanied by her husband, but before she consulted me, he had changed his job and was no longer able to take her, so she felt stranded.

We used the affect bridge technique to help her make sense of her anxiety attacks. First I asked her to focus on where she felt the anxiety, and she pinpointed her chest and all over her body. She became hot, her hands sweated, she felt palpitations and believed she couldn't get enough air.

I then asked her to imagine she was in the supermarket and feel the feeling. When she had achieved that, I counted slowly from 50 back to nought and she nodded to indicate that the feeling increased at the ages of 35, 30 and 20. We then discussed what had happened to her during those years.

'At 20 my fiancé broke off our engagement. I was devastated. I couldn't stop crying and couldn't see any future for me. He was the man of my dreams and he went off with someone else. I panicked, became depressed and couldn't cope.'

She sobbed as she recalled this traumatic experience, indicating that those intense emotions were still unresolved.

'At 30 I lost my job. I didn't know if we could make ends meet. I was married by then but we needed two incomes to pay the bills. I felt out of control and guilty. I worried day and night and had those terrible feelings again. After a few months I found another job and things returned to an even keel.

'At 35 I got a terrible fright when I was shopping and someone tried to grab my bag. They didn't get it but I felt awful for days and worried in case it happened again. I got those feelings again, the ones I get when I'm alone at the supermarket.'

Lucy and I used the information she had gained from the affect bridge to add reason to her emotions. She was basically an anxious person, so it was not easy to convince her to let go of her fears. We used other techniques, such as visualisation (see below) to replace the anxiety with calmness; we arranged outings to the supermarket with her husband, where she was in control and could focus on positive feelings while shopping; she learned relaxation techniques; we talked about the past experiences from 20, 30 and 35 in order to release and resolve them, and eventually she was able to shop without panic attacks.

Visualisation

Imagining, which is what visualisation consists of, has been shown to be a very powerful force that influences many systems in the mind/body complex. For example, just imagining your hand in cold water can lower the skin temperature by several degrees.

We all use our imagination during the day (and at night in dreams) to create positive or negative feelings. Imagining that the plane we are going to travel on might crash will create fear, while imagining the holiday experience we are going to have will create happiness. Imagination and emotions are inextricably linked.

Visualisation is not related to logic or rationality. In fact, illogical, strange or crazy images are likely to be the most effective in creating change. As in dreaming, we are using unconscious sources to improve our feelings. The only rule is not to try: simply be, observe and accept. Do not question or analyse – just allow whatever happens to happen. Trying lifts us back into the conscious mind and so nullifies our aim.

The only other requirement of visualisation is quiet time, when we are not under pressure from anyone or anything else. Use this quiet time to imagine what it would be like to change or improve a particular feeling.

How to use visualisation

1. Take a little while to relax in an unhurried, undisturbed place and time.
2. Focus on the feeling, as in the affect bridge technique. Sense where it is in the body, what colour and shape it has, whether it is moving or still, heavy or light, bright or dull, quiet or accompanied by sounds, tight or loose.
3. Focus on what you would like to have there instead. Again, see the colour, shape and other qualities of the replacement.
4. Notice how the new configuration feels. Keep adapting it until the feeling is the one you wish to create.
5. Imagine the situation that caused the original feeling and create the picture you want to be associated with that experience. This allows you to break the bond between experience and picture and replace it with a new link. The new link will create an improved experience/feeling connection.

Case History

Katie got a feeling of dread whenever she met her uncle. She doesn't like him but feels obliged to visit. He has been mean and unkind to her in the past, but her parents insist that she takes her children to see him because he is getting old. Her aim was to reduce the dread so that her visits wouldn't be such a nightmare.

We went through the steps outlined above. First Katie sat quietly with her eyes closed for a little while. Next she 'went inside' with a 'being' attitude rather than a 'trying' one. Next she focused on the dread feeling, which was in her abdomen. She described it as black, heavy, tight, of no particular shape, soundless and empty.

The feeling she wanted was one of calmness, and she described this as light in colour and weight, bright, gently moving and loose. She spent some minutes focusing on the new colours and shapes until she felt the calmness she desired. She then imagined meeting her uncle, and the colour and shape immediately changed back to those of dread.

We discussed this change and she realised the power of the link between experience and internal picture. She agreed to practise at home every night, desensitising herself from the association between uncle visits and dread and replacing it with calm.

After a number of weeks and further support, Katie was able to make the change and could imagine visiting her uncle and remaining calm. She agreed to put the exercise to the test on her next visit. It was a partial success: her dread was reduced from 100 to 50, and she was able to maintain part of the calm composition for some of the time.

Katie believed that if she continued to work at it, the calm would grow and the dread would shrink even further.

The technique of visualisation can be utilised in many different ways. In cancer therapy some patients have been helped by imagining sharks eating the cancer cells, while migraine sufferers have reduced the incidence of headaches by imagining they are wearing an ice helmet to keep a cool head. In other contexts imagining past experiences and future aims can create confidence and the will-power to change. Similarly, relaxation procedures may use symbols and images to improve perspective. The only limitation is your own creativity.

Visualising the projectionist

If a client is having nightmares, or images of future or past events are causing unwanted emotions, I use this technique to learn about the unconscious mechanism in order to make an improvement.

1. Sit quietly and imagine you are in a cinema. See a blank screen in front of you.
2. Now see the images on the screen that have been causing the problem.
3. Imagine getting up from your seat and walking to the back of the cinema towards the projectionist's room.
4. Open the door of the projectionist's room and see the projector running and showing the film.
5. See who is in charge of the projector: it may be someone you know, or a character you have never seen before. It doesn't matter who it is as long as your imagination rather than your rational mind is in charge.
6. Ask the person if they are showing the film, and if so, for what purpose. Explain to them that the film is causing problems; it is out of date and is not helpful. Negotiate with the projectionist to destroy or change the film to one you prefer.
7. If there are difficulties in the negotiation, point out that he is a tenant in your mind: you are the landlord and have authority.
8. When a new, improved film is running, thank the projectionist, go back to your seat and note how you feel with the new film.

You may need to repeat the technique a number of times to overcome previous patterns. The new film needs to create the feeling you wish to have.

Case History

Martin was ten years old when his mother brought him to see me. His problem was recurrent nightmares that had been happening for some months. He had been bullied at school and his mother believed there was some connection between this and his bad dreams.

Martin and I discussed both his bullying and the dreams,

and he was happy to see if we could improve both. I mentioned that dreams are films in the mind, and Martin closed his eyes and imagined he was in a cinema watching these films.

He went to the back of the theatre and opened the projectionist's door. The projectionist was an old man with a beard. When asked why he was showing the frightening films, he said, 'I'm just obeying the master.'

'Could we speak to the master?' I asked.

Another man appeared, who was older and smaller. He confirmed that he was directing the projectionist to show the films.

There was some discussion between Martin and the master, and an agreement was made to show better films that would not produce fear. Martin then went back to his seat and watched films that were calming and helped his confidence.

After the session Martin's mother and I discussed ways to help deal with the bullying.

At the next visit Martin's nightmares had stopped completely, and he believed that the projectionist exercise played a major role in achieving this.

Visualising the child within

One of the most powerful visualisation techniques is called 'helping the child within'. It is based on the idea that many of our thoughts, actions and emotions are governed by what we learnt during childhood. For example, if a child has a traumatic experience, such as being jumped on by a dog, the fear experienced at the time may continue into adulthood as a dog phobia. It is as if the child within is dictating how the adult acts and feels. The child is stuck in a time warp, where it is reasonable for small children to be frightened of a big dog. However, it is unreasonable for an adult to have the same degree of fear.

Visualisation and quiet time are used to 'go inside' the feeling and return to the time when it first developed (the affect bridge).

Contact is then made with the child who had the original experience.

The adult then becomes the therapist to the child. Visualising the adult and child together, with the adult being supportive, caring, understanding and informing, helps to resolve the original emotions. The adult has knowledge and power that the child does not possess. In the dog scenario, for example, the child might feel he is about to die, but the adult (you) knows this doesn't happen because you are still alive. Informing the child of this fact allows him to let go of the terror of death. By spending time with the child within, out-of-date, inaccurate or unhelpful emotions can be calmed and replaced by more helpful ones. In this way the child is integrated into the adult.

1. Have quiet time to do the exercise.
2. Focus on the feeling you wish to change.
3. Using your imagination, go back in time to the first experience you can remember when that feeling occurred.
4. Imagine the younger you who is having that experience living in the part of your body where the feeling is located.
5. Have your adult self present with you as the child.
6. Your role as the adult is to gain trust, take time, listen and inform the child about things it wishes to know.
7. Allow this communication to have a life of its own so that the child and the adult can communicate.

Repeat this exercise on a regular basis until the feeling has been integrated and become more helpful.

Case History

Ben was 30 and in distress because he was to be the best man at a wedding in two months' time. His worst fear in the world was public speaking, and he was desperate for help with an event that he could not avoid.

Basically shy, unconfident and anxious, Ben spent much of

his time avoiding circumstances that would force him to behave differently. On a one-to-one basis he could cope reasonably well, but parties where he didn't know anyone were a nightmare, so he had developed many excuses to avoid them.

He said he had always been frightened of speaking in a group, even as far back as the age of ten when he had to recite poetry in class and forgot the words.

We discussed his belief systems and fears, and focused on the speech that lay ahead. Then we went through the steps outlined above.

First I helped him to relax. He said that the feeling of fear was in his chest: it was tight, made his heart race and felt very uncomfortable. He labelled it 'terror'.

Focusing on the tight feeling in his chest, he went back in time to the ten-year-old reciting poetry in class. He imagined the ten-year-old living in his chest.

Next he went into his chest as the 30-year-old so that he could comfort the ten-year-old and put the situation into perspective. He spent some minutes communicating with the child through feelings rather than logic. He listened, supported, gave confidence and told the child about the wonderful things that would happen in the future.

He helped the child within to realise that it was not such an important event to forget the words in a poetry recital, that it was normal, that everyone at some stage had that experience. He showed the little boy that those few seconds were a very small part of his life and that he didn't need to carry the feeling they caused into the future. This made the anxious child inside become calmer and happier.

Over the next two weeks Ben repeated this exercise and realised that neither the poetry recital nor the wedding speech need cause the fear he had been experiencing. Neither experience carried much significance and he could feel comfortable with both.

In the run-up to the wedding Ben put his speech into perspective. He talked to the child within during the day and discussed what was happening with his daily routine. He said it was like having an internal friend to share things with.

Ben's speech went well, helped by the fact that he was surrounded by friends who had been drinking for some time before he performed. He told me he would keep talking to the child within because it improved his confidence a great deal, and helped him to realise that many of the things he gave importance to really didn't matter.

Listening to Your Body

The body is constantly sending us messages, many of which we take for granted or choose to ignore. Sometimes we deliberately block them out by using alcohol, cigarettes or medication. While these tactics may work for a while, it is actually more helpful and productive to listen to your body. Just as a car mechanic listens to an engine to detect and repair faults, so we too can 'detect and repair faults' by listening to our bodies.

While it is important to respond to bodily sensations, it is also important to distinguish them from the underlying cause.

Case History

Delia was 70 when she consulted me for a 'terrible low feeling' she had experienced for six months. She had taken many tablets and had a number of tests, but the feeling persisted.

Delia lived alone, Brownie, her cocker spaniel of 12 years, having died a year previously. Delia wondered if the low feeling was associated with his death. She had not discussed this with doctors because she didn't want to 'waste their time', and obediently took their tablets although she doubted they would be of any help.

As we discussed her low feeling, it became apparent to both of us that it was her body's message that she was grieving for Brownie. I therefore directed her to a bereavement counsellor who works with people who have lost pets. There she received help for the problem rather than the message, and after a few weeks the counsellor wrote to tell me that Delia was feeling much better and the low feeling had diminished.

As with many other techniques, listening to your body requires quiet time. This allows you to focus inwards without distraction and be aware of the bodily sensations that are occurring. It should be done on a daily basis for about ten minutes.

Many people claim that they don't have time for introspection, and would rather take a tablet. To them I point out that to overcome difficulties we must take responsibility for our lives, and put in time and effort. A tablet will temporarily block messages and feelings, but the problem will remain.

The ten-minute quiet time each day involves 'going inside' and being aware of any bodily sensations you feel. These can be many and varied, perhaps relating to physical exercise you have performed, emotional experiences registering in your body, tension from external pressure, or guilt from past experiences.

With your eyes closed focus inwards and circumnavigate your body, noticing how the different parts feel. Don't try and change any, but be aware of what the feelings are even if they are uncomfortable. When you have completed this circumnavigation, be open to any messages that may come from these feelings: what are they trying to tell you? For example, 'I notice a tightness in my jaw. As I focus on it I recall the conflict I have been experiencing about decisions I need to make at work.'

This process helps you to realise that the tightness is a symptom rather than a problem, a sign directing you to resolve the conflict. By spending quiet time focusing on this issue you are respecting the underlying message, even though you may not be able to resolve the conflict. This recognition generally allows the tension to be reduced.

By listening to your body on a daily basis, you will become more adept at noticing bodily messages when they occur. This means that your mind/body connection becomes a continuous one, allowing you to respond at the time you receive the message.

The Importance of Breathing

It may seem obvious, or even odd, to say that breathing is important. After all, we know what would happen if we stopped. The important thing, though, is to breathe correctly and realise when you are breathing incorrectly.

Breathing serves two functions: it provides the body with oxygen and it removes carbon dioxide (a waste product). It is the latter that causes problems when we breathe incorrectly: the carbon dioxide level in the body falls if we overbreathe (hyperventilate), and this produces many symptoms, including headaches, tiredness, panic attacks, sweating and hand muscle spasms.

Correct breathing comes from the diaphragm, which moves up and down, causing the abdomen to move in and out. The normal rate of breathing is 12–14 breaths a minute. When relaxed, the rate may drop to 6–7 breaths per minute.

Incorrect breathing tends to use the chest muscles and be fast, shallow and irregular. However, breathing too deeply is also incorrect because it expels too much carbon dioxide.

Breathing is an unusual mechanism because it is under the control of both the conscious and unconscious minds. This means that it occurs automatically without our awareness, but we can, if we wish to, influence the rate or depth of breathing. The need to breathe is so powerful that it overrides any other drive we may have, even if the circumstances are not conducive to breathing – say, under water or when enveloped by flames.

There is an intricate relationship between breathing and

emotions. Overbreathing will change our emotions and powerful emotions will affect our breathing. An anxious person broadcasts his emotion by rapid breathing, while an angry person expels air sharply and a sad person sighs excessively.

People who have panic attacks nearly always hyperventilate (breathe excessively and with their chest). They say their feelings tell them they can't get enough air, but the opposite is true. Treatment is aimed at reducing their anxiety and teaching them to breathe correctly. An excellent book by Deanna Bradley, *The Hyperventilation Syndrome*, explains every aspect of this condition, which is becoming more widely recognised.

While breathing can cause problems, it can also provide the solution. When feeling anxious we can create calmness by breathing 'slow and low'. Slowing the respiratory rate and using the diaphragm allows the carbon dioxide level to return to normal and restore calmness. (It surprises me that the advice to take deep breaths when you are anxious is still given because it is quite wrong: it is not intrinsically calming – it merely serves as a distraction from the anxiety.)

By being aware of your breathing, recognising when it is incorrect and changing the pattern to one that is slow and low you are learning about the most basic activity of the mind/body system. This awareness allows you to control many of the processes occurring in your body, reduce overwhelming emotions, create calmness and confidence, and become aware of the connection between breathing and your emotional state.

Conclusion

'Actions have outcomes, and we need to take
responsibility for our actions.'
BRIAN ROET

When I started writing this book I approached the subject as a
naturalist might approach a specific part of an ecosystem. I
needed to look not only at the emotional component, but also
at how it affected the mind/body system as a whole.

My research took me in many different directions, and answers
often prompted further questions. Each piece of understanding
I gained connected me to another aspect of the ecosystem I was
exploring. The challenge was that neither the subject nor the
specific components were static: the emotions and the mind/body
system are in constant interaction with each other.

I have tried to explain different aspects of emotion so that
you the reader will be able to identify your habits and needs,
and make practical use of the information and advice I provide.
You might need to refer back to specific chapters as different
experiences occur in your life. If you have read the book slowly
and thoughtfully, you will notice that changes sometimes occur
quickly when you are struck by a new idea, but generally changes
take time – two steps forward and one step back. By being aware
of your attitudes, thoughts, remarks and feelings you are in the
best position to make those improvements. In the words of Ron
Barassi, a famous Australian rules football coach, 'If it is to be,
it is up to me.'

Readers of self-help books usually fall into two categories. The first read the book, declare it very interesting, then put it on a shelf and think no more about it. The second read the book and decide to do something about their lives, making time and effort to put some of the thoughts, techniques and advice into practice.

The readers in category one are taking an action where there will be no change, their lives will be more of the same, and problems/barriers will continue to prevent them achieving their aims. The readers in category two will be the beneficiaries of what I have written. They will convert the written word into a thought or action, they will 'have a go', learn from their mistakes and move forward so that life will be easier, more successful, more rewarding. I do hope that you and the majority of readers will fall into the second category and learn to harness the energy and power that your emotions possess. In that way conflicts will be reduced and you will learn to trust your feelings as friends, to guide you in the best possible way for your mind/body ecosystem to thrive.

Further Information

For those who enjoy receiving information through the spoken word, Dr Roet has made a tape to accompany this book. Side A deals with understanding emotions, and Side B gives practical techniques for quiet time.

To purchase this tape send a cheque for £10.00 made payable to Dr Roet to:

Dr Brian Roet
2 The Mews
6 Putney Common
London
SW15 1HL
Telephone: 020 8780 2284

Further Reading

Developing Intuition, Shakti Gawain (New World Library, 2000)

Emotional Blackmail, Susan Forward (Bantam Books, 1997)

Emotional Intelligence, Daniel Goldman (Bloomsbury Publications, 1996)

Emotion: the Sequence of Sentiment, Dylan Evans (Oxford University Press, 2001)

The Feeling of What Happens, Antonio Damasio (Vintage Publications, 2000)

Healing the Whole Person, Robert McNeilly (John Wiley & Sons, 2000)

The Hyperventilation Syndrome, Deanna Bradley (Kyle Cathie Publishers, 2000)

Men Are from Mars, Women Are from Venus, John Gray (Thorsons, 1992)

Mind over Mood, Dennis Greenberger and Christine Padesky (Guildhall Press, 1992)

Molecules of Emotion, Candice Pert (Pocket Books, 1997)

The Sensuous Garden, Monty Don (Conran Octopus, 1997)

Trusting the Tides, Anne Dickson (Rider Books, 2000)

The 20-Minute Break, Ernest L. Rossi (Zeig, Tucker & Theisen, 1991)

Who Moved My Cheese?, Spencer Johnson (Vermilion, 1999)

Working with Your Chakras, Ruth White (Piatkus Books, 1993)

Index

Note: page numbers in **bold** refer to illustrations.